TEXT BY CRISTINA BANFI

BITE-SIZED FACTS
NATURE

whitestar kids

CONTENTS

ANIMALS

PLANTS AND MUSHROOMS

HABITATS

EARTH

DO YOU HAVE 5 MINUTES?

NATURE IS IMPORTANT BECAUSE IT IS ALL AROUND US AND OUR VERY EXISTENCE DEPENDS ON IT.

WE ADMIRE ITS BEAUTY, MARVEL AT ITS PERFECTION, AND ENJOY ITS GENEROUS GIFTS.

IF WE CAN UNDERSTAND NATURE, WE CAN CREATE A SPECIAL BOND WITH IT AND DEVELOP A DEEP AND LASTING RESPECT FOR THE NATURAL ENVIRONMENT.

You surely already know this, but maybe you think that you do not have enough time to get to know nature better.

We'll let you in on a secret: It takes only 5 minutes to make amazing discoveries about the natural world! Does that seem too quick? Put yourself to the test!

YOU CAN DEVELOP AN IN-DEPTH KNOWLEDGE OF HOW NATURE WORKS AROUND YOU IN AN EASY, FUN, AND FAST WAY. IN FACT, THERE IS A LOT OF INFORMATION IN THIS BOOK, AND YOUR SKILLS WILL GROW IN SMALL DOSES JUST BY READING A FEW SENTENCES AT A TIME.

By flipping through these pages you can light a fuse that will set off your curiosity, which, as we know, is the most powerful engine for learning.

IT DOESN'T MATTER IF YOU DON'T HAVE A LOT OF TIME OR A SUFFICIENT ATTENTION SPAN: IMAGES AND SHORT PARAGRAPHS WILL REVEAL, IN THE BLINK OF AN EYE, FACTS AND TRIVIA YOU COULDN'T EVEN IMAGINE.

YOU'LL LEARN ABOUT PLANTS, BIRDS, FISH, TREES, AND ECOSYSTEMS, AND IF YOU STILL WONDER ABOUT THINGS LIKE, "WHAT ARE AMPHIBIANS? HOW DO MOUNTAINS FORM? WHY ARE BEES IMPORTANT?" NO PROBLEM! WE ARE SURE YOU WILL FIND A SUPER QUICK ANSWER TO YOUR QUESTIONS WITHIN THE PAGES.

Devote the next 5 MINUTES to reading... and enjoy!

ANIMALS

-Chapter 1-

PETS

They are animals that have been bred and that have adapted to live with humans.

Over time, their DNA has changed, and today it is different from that of their ancestors or wild "cousins."

14,000 years ago

DOGS HAVE BEEN MAN'S BEST FRIEND SINCE BEFORE FARMING BEGAN. IN 2016, A STUDY FOUND THAT THEIR DOMESTICATION OCCURRED 14,000 YEARS AGO IN TWO DIFFERENT PLACES: EUROPE AND EAST ASIA.

Pet GOATS

GOATS WERE PROBABLY THE FIRST ANIMALS TO BE RAISED BY HUMANS, MAINLY FOR THEIR NUTRITIOUS MILK.

Laughing HORSES?

HORSES ARE BRED MAINLY FOR THEIR STRENGTH AND RUNNING ABILITY. SOMETIMES IT MAY SEEM AS THOUGH A HORSE IS LAUGHING. THIS IS ACTUALLY A REACTION TO CERTAIN SMELLS IN THE AIR.

100,000

IT IS ESTIMATED THAT A DOG'S SENSE OF SMELL IS 100,000 TIMES GREATER THAN A HUMAN'S.

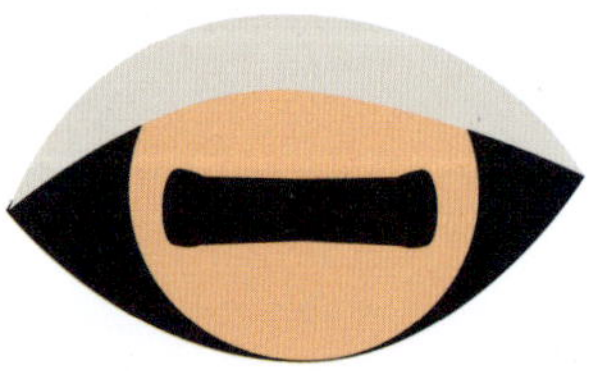

YOU WOULD HAVE A HARD TIME SURPRISING A SHEEP OR GOAT FROM BEHIND; THEIR EYES HAVE A FIELD OF VISION OF MORE THAN 300 DEGREES, ALLOWING THEM TO SEE BEHIND THEM WITHOUT HAVING TO MOVE THEIR HEADS.

ENGLISH COCKER SPANIEL

THESE HUNTING DOGS (THEY ALSO HUNT FOR TURFFLES) ARE EXCELLENT SWIMMERS.

COW friends

COWS HAVE A MEMORY THAT LASTS ABOUT THREE YEARS AND ARE ABLE TO RECOGNIZE THEIR OWN NAMES. THEY ARE VERY SOCIABLE ANIMALS AND FORM LASTING FRIENDSHIP BONDS WITH OTHER COWS.

Fast PIGS

PIGS CAN RUN MORE THAN 10 MILES PER HOUR (ALMOST AS FAST AS A PERSON RIDING A BICYCLE). THEY HAVE NO SWEAT GLANDS, SO IF THEY GET HOT THEY HAVE TO ROLL IN MUD TO STAY COOL.

Very BIG TEETH!

RABBITS' TEETH GROW CONTINUOUSLY, ALMOST HALF AN INCH (UP TO A CENTIMETER) A MONTH, ALTHOUGH THE HARD HAY THEY EAT HELPS TO FILE THEM DOWN.

Egyptians CATS

CATS EVERYWHERE ARE DESCENDED FROM A FEW DOMESTICATED INDIVIDUALS IN ANCIENT EGYPT MORE THAN 3,000 YEARS AGO. FROM THERE THEY SPREAD AROUND THE WORLD THROUGH TRADE ROUTES.

PERSIAN CAT

THIS IS A PEACEFUL DOMESTIC CAT NATIVE TO ASIA MINOR.

FELINES

Felines are born to hunt!

They all have keen senses, agile bodies, sharp teeth, powerful jaws, and sharp claws, plus they are excellent climbers and skilled swimmers!

ROAR OR PURR?

BIG CATS, SUCH AS THE LION, TIGER, JAGUAR, AND LEOPARD, CAN ROAR BUT THEY CANNOT PURR. THE SMALL CATS IN THIS FAMILY, ALONG WITH COUGARS AND CHEETAHS, CAN PURR BUT THEY DO NOT ROAR!

Retractable CLAWS

FELINE CLAWS CAN BE RETRACTED INSIDE THE PAW TO PROTECT THEM FROM WEAR AND TEAR. THE ONLY EXCEPTION IS THE CHEETAH, WHICH ALWAYS HAS THEM EXPOSED FOR MORE GRIP WITH THE GROUND WHILE RUNNING.

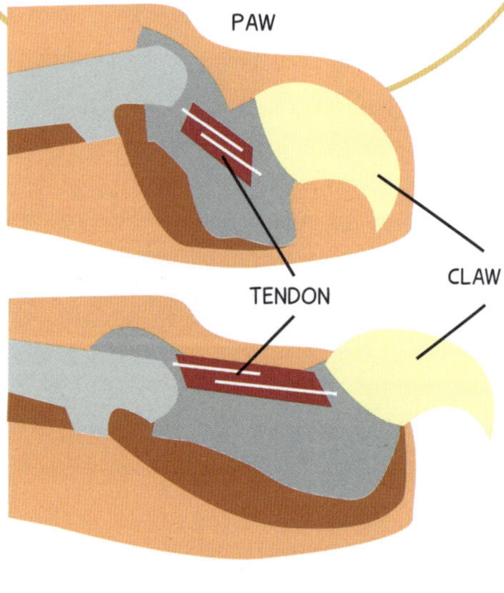

What BIG TEETH!

THE SMILODON, A HUGE FELINE THAT LIVED IN PREHISTORIC TIMES, WAS ALSO KNOWN AS THE SABER-TOOTHED TIGER BECAUSE OF ITS EXCEPTIONALLY LONG CANINES.

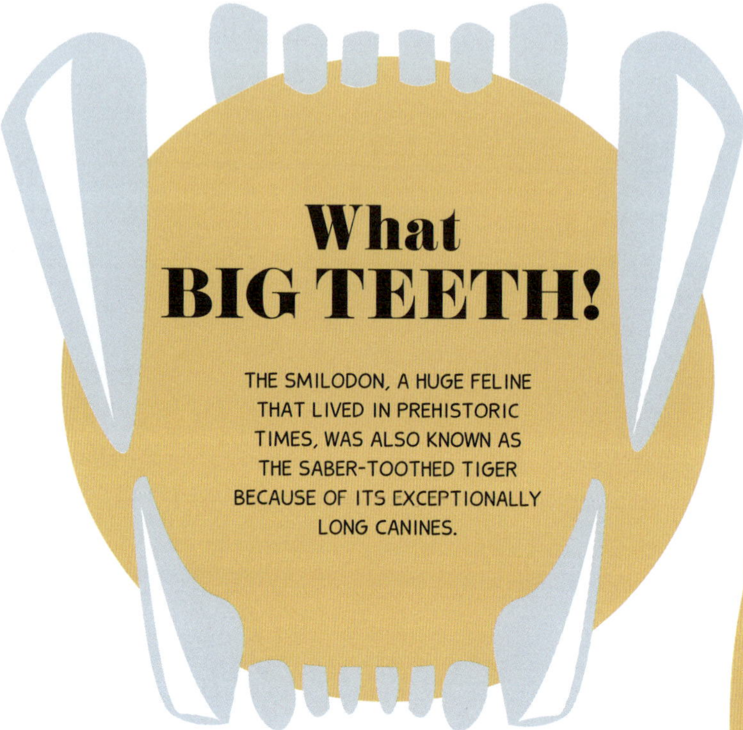

EYES

AS WITH MANY PREDATORS, FELINES' EYES FACE FORWARD FOR BINOCULAR VISION. THIS IS WHY THEY CAN JUDGE THE DISTANCE TO THINGS VERY WELL WHEN HUNTING, CLIMBING, AND JUMPING.

FELINES' EYES APPEAR TO GLOW IN THE DARK BECAUSE THEY HAVE AN ADDITIONAL LAYER OF TISSUE INSIDE CALLED A SHINY MAT THAT REFLECTS EVEN THE FAINTEST LIGHT AND ENHANCES NIGHT VISION.

Quiet QUIET...

MOST FELINES RELY ON STEALTH: THEY SILENTLY APPROACH THEIR PREY UNTIL THEY ARE CLOSE ENOUGH TO MAKE A FINAL, DEADLY LEAP.

The LARGEST...

THE LARGEST LIVING FELINE SPECIES IS THE SIBERIAN TIGER. MALES CAN REACH WEIGHTS OF UP TO 660 LB (300 KG) AND A LENGTH FROM NOSE TO TAIL APPROACHING 13 FT (4 M).

...and the SMALLEST

IS THE RUSTY-SPOTTED CAT, WHICH IS MORE PETITE THAN EVEN A HOUSE CAT, WEIGHING ABOUT 3.3 LB (1.5 KG).

JAGUAR

THIS IS THE THIRD LARGEST FELINE IN THE WORLD, AND IT LIVES MAINLY IN THE AMAZON REGION. THERE ARE ALSO VARIETIES WITH COMPLETELY BLACK FUR CALLED PANTHERS!

46

THE NUMBER OF SPECIES IN THE FELINE FAMILY, NATIVE TO ALL AREAS OF THE WORLD EXCEPT AUSTRALIA AND ANTARCTICA.

AMPHIBIANS

They have a special bond with water, and they can never be too far away from it.

Zoologists divide amphibians into three major groups: frogs and toads; salamanders and newts; and caecilians, which, having a long, thin body and lacking legs, closely resemble large worms.

370 MILION years ago

AMPHIBIANS APPEARED ON EARTH ABOUT 370 MILLION YEARS AGO. THEIR ANCESTORS WERE FISH WITH FLESHY FINS. THEY ARE CONSIDERED THE FIRST LAND ANIMALS.

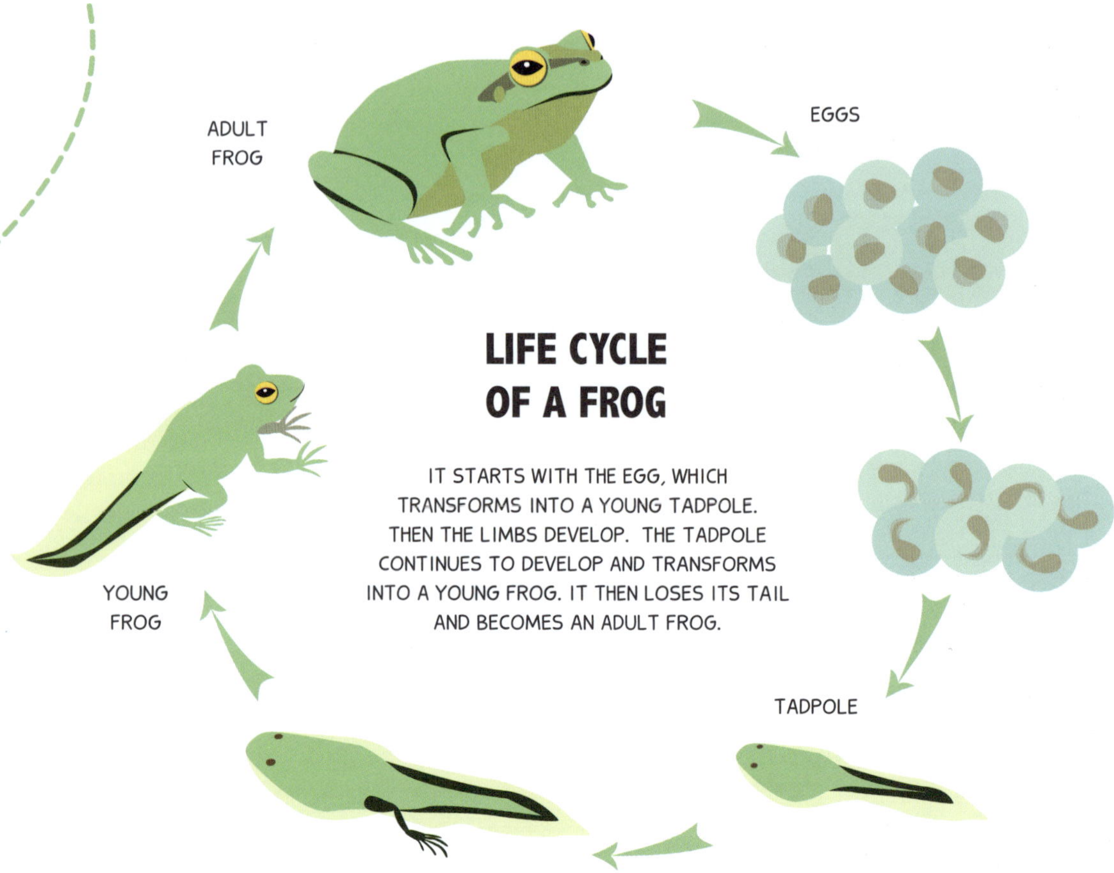

LIFE CYCLE OF A FROG

IT STARTS WITH THE EGG, WHICH TRANSFORMS INTO A YOUNG TADPOLE. THEN THE LIMBS DEVELOP. THE TADPOLE CONTINUES TO DEVELOP AND TRANSFORMS INTO A YOUNG FROG. IT THEN LOSES ITS TAIL AND BECOMES AN ADULT FROG.

RECORD!

THE LARGEST FROG IN THE WORLD IS THE GOLIATH FROG, WHICH CAN WEIGH UP TO 7.2 LB (3.3 KG) AND MEASURE 11.8 IN (30 CM)!

WHILE THE SMALLEST FROG IN THE WORLD IS THE *LIMNONECTES PHYLLOFOLIA*, WHICH IS 0.3 IN (7.7 MM) LONG.

Obstetric TOAD

THE MALE MIDWIFE TOAD DEVOTES HIMSELF TO CARING FOR THE EGGS. HE STRAPS THE GELATINOUS STRING OF EGGS ON HIS HIND LEGS AND KEEPS IT WITH HIM FOR ABOUT A MONTH UNTIL HATCHING.

So much MUCUS!

MANY AMPHIBIANS ALSO BREATHE THROUGH THEIR SKIN, WHICH IS VERY THIN. THE SKIN IS KEPT MOIST AT ALL TIMES BY MUCUS PRODUCED BY NUMEROUS GLANDS.

8,500

THE NUMBER OF SPECIES OF AMPHIBIANS CURRENTLY KNOWN IN THE WORLD, OF WHICH MORE THAN 7,600 ARE FROGS AND TOADS.

Forever TADPOLE

SOME SPECIES REMAIN TADPOLES THROUGHOUT THEIR LIVES. SUCH IS THE CASE WITH THE AXOLOTL, WHICH RETAINS ITS DORSAL FIN AND HAS FEATHERY GILLS ON THE SIDES OF ITS HEAD.

UH-UH-UH

TO ATTRACT FEMALES DURING THE BREEDING SEASON, FROGS AND TOADS EMIT A CALL. IN THE CASE OF THE LITTLE HOWLER TOAD (*BOMBINA* SPP.), THE SOUND IS UNMISTAKABLE: A FAINT, REGULAR "UH-UH-UH" THAT ECHOES RHYTHMICALLY IN THE AIR.

TOXIC skin

THERE ARE OFTEN GLANDS ON THE SKIN OF AMPHIBIANS THAT PRODUCE TOXIC OR UNPLEASANT SUBSTANCES USEFUL IN DETERRING PREDATORS.

JAVAN TREE FROG

THIS FROG CAN GLIDE, THANKS TO THE LARGE MEMBRANES BETWEEN ITS TOES. WHEN OPENED AT THE MOMENT OF JUMPING, THEY PRODUCE A PARACHUTE EFFECT.

REPTILES

Millions of years ago, reptiles ruled the world.

They may have a forked tongue, sharp teeth, or skin covered with scales that is mistakenly thought to be slimy. They live just about everywhere-some in water, others on land, at ground level, or in trees.

6,000

THE NUMBER OF REPTILE SPECIES KNOWN TODAY, INCLUDING CROCODILES, ALLIGATORS, GHARIALS, TURTLES, TORTOISES, LIZARDS, AND SNAKES.

20 minutes

THE BLACK MAMBA'S VENOMOUS BITE CAN KILL A PERSON IN 20 MINUTES.

WHITE-LIPPED VIPER

TRIMERESURUS ALBOLABRIS IS A VENOMOUS PIT VIPER SPECIES ENDEMIC TO SOUTHEAST ASIA.

Brrr

ALL REPTILES ARE COLD-BLOODED-THAT IS, THEY ADJUST THEIR BODY TEMPERATURE TO THAT OF THE ENVIRONMENT, SO THEY NEED TO SUPPLY THEMSELVES WITH HEAT BY BASKING IN THE SUN DURING THE DAY.

340 MILION years ago

THE FIRST REPTILES APPEARED, EVOLVING DIRECTLY FROM AMPHIBIANS. REPTILES HAVE THE ADVANTAGE OF TOUGH SKIN THAT DOES NOT DRY OUT IN THE AIR, AND MOST ARE BORN FROM EGGS EQUIPPED WITH HARD SHELLS.

3 EYES

THE TUATARA HAS REAL SUPERPOWERS: IT CAN WITHSTAND EXTREMELY COLD TEMPERATURES AND HOLD ITS BREATH FOR AN HOUR, AND IT HAS A THIRD EYE ON ITS FOREHEAD WITH WHICH IT SENSES CHANGES IN BRIGHTNESS.

ANYWHERE

THANKS TO FINGERTIPS FORMED BY 6.5 MILLION MICROSCOPIC HOOKS, GECKOS CAN SCALE ANY SURFACE!

IT WON'T sink!

THE CHARACTERISTIC FEATURE OF THE FEATHERED BASILISK IS THAT IT CAN RUN ON WATER FOR UP TO 16.4 FT (5 M) DUE TO AN ADAPTATION OF ITS HIND LEGS, WHICH TRAP SMALL AIR BUBBLES. THESE FAST MOVEMENTS ALLOW THE LIZARD TO REACH SPEEDS OF 6.21 MILES PER HOUR (10 KM/H).

60 days

THE NUMBER OF DAYS IT TAKES TO REGROW A TAIL! MANY LIZARD SPECIES DROP THEIR TAILS AS A DEFENSE MECHANISM. THE PREDATOR, IN FACT, IS DISTRACTED BY THE SURPRISE, ALLOWING THE LIZARD TO ESCAPE.

INSECTS

There is no terrestrial environment where they are not present.

Insects are invertebrates-that is, they do not have an internal skeleton. They do, however, have a tough, protective exoskeleton that covers the entire body.

So MANY

ACCORDING TO CURRENT ESTIMATES OF SCIENTISTS, 90 PERCENT OF ANIMALS ON EARTH ARE INSECTS.

Something IN COMMON

INSECTS ARE THE MOST DIVERSE GROUP OF ANIMALS ON EARTH, YET THEY ALL HAVE COMMON CHARACTERISTICS: THEIR BODIES CONSIST OF THREE PARTS (A HEAD, A THORAX, AND AN ABDOMEN), THEY HAVE SIX LEGS, MOST HAVE COMPOUND EYES, AND MANY HAVE WINGS.

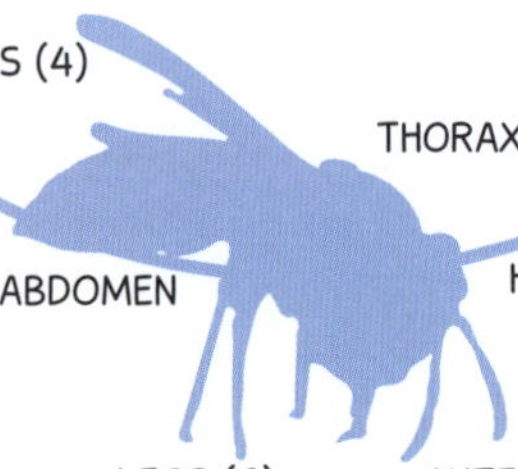

More than 1.5 MILLION

THE NUMBER OF INSECT SPECIES DISCOVERED SO FAR, BUT SCIENTISTS AGREE THAT MANY ARE YET TO BE DISCOVERED.

No LUNGS!

ON AN INSECT'S ABDOMEN, WHICH CONTAINS THE INTERNAL ORGANS, ARE THE OPENINGS OF TINY TUBES CALLED TRACHEAE, WHICH INSECTS NEED TO BREATHE.

Even in ANTARCTICA

EVEN THE ANTARCTIC CONTINENT IS HOME TO INSECTS. THERE ARE A FEW SPECIES OF SMALL FLIES, THE ONLY ANIMALS THAT LIVE THERE PERMANENTLY.

DRAGONFLY

THE DRAGONFLY CAN PERFORM SPECTACULAR FLYING STUNTS, THANKS TO ITS ABILITY TO MOVE ITS FOUR WINGS INDEPENDENTLY OF EACH OTHER.

ESSENTIAL

ALTHOUGH SOME SPECIES CAN BE HARMFUL, INSECTS ARE VALUABLE ANIMALS BECAUSE THEY PLAY AN IMPORTANT ROLE AS POLLINATORS, AS DECOMPOSERS, AND IN THE FOOD CHAIN BECAUSE THEY ARE A SOURCE OF FOOD FOR SO MANY OTHER ANIMALS.

Compound EYES

THEY ARE CALLED THIS BECAUSE THEY ARE MADE UP OF INDIVIDUAL SIDE-BY-SIDE UNITS IN NUMBERS RANGING FROM A FEW DOZEN TO THOUSANDS.

What COLORS!

THE RANGE OF COLORS PERCEIVED BY INSECTS IS HUGE, INCLUDING SOME NOT PERCEIVED BY THE HUMAN EYE, SUCH AS ULTRAVIOLET COLORS

At BIRTH

ALL INSECTS ARE BORN FROM EGGS. IN SOME SPECIES THE BABIES ARE LIKE MINIATURE ADULTS, WHILE IN OTHERS THEY MUST GO THROUGH SEVERAL STAGES, FROM LARVAE TO PUPAE THAT REST IN A COCOON UNTIL THEY BECOME ADULTS.

Patient LARVAE

THE LARVAE OF SOME CICADA SPECIES LIVE UNDERGROUND FOR 17 YEARS.

BEES

In a single collecting trip, a bee visits 50 to 100 flowers.

Surely you are very familiar with bees. They are the small yellow-and-black banded insects that are often seen flying from flower to flower. Less well known is that there are different kinds of bees. Some are wild and solitary, others don't sting but do bite, and still others are bred by humans in exchange for the sweetest honey.

5 EYES

BEES HAVE FIVE EYES, TWO COMPOUND AND THREE SIMPLE, WITH WHICH THEY CAN SEE ALL COLORS EXCEPT RED.

2 MILLION years ago

THE EUROPEAN HONEYBEE APPEARED ABOUT 2 MILLION YEARS AGO AND TODAY IS THE MOST WIDESPREAD BEE IN THE WORLD, WITH 26 RECOGNIZED SUBSPECIES.

3300

THE AGE OF THE OLDEST JAR OF HONEY IN THE WORLD, WHICH WAS FOUND INSIDE AN EGYPTIAN TOMB AND IS STILL PERFECTLY EDIBLE!

HIVE

AN AVERAGE HIVE CAN HOUSE ABOUT 50,000 BEES. WITHIN IT THERE IS A STRICT DIVISION OF LABOR, AND EACH BEE COOPERATES FOR THE WELFARE OF ALL. INSIDE THERE ARE HONEYCOMBS, BUILT BY BEES FROM WAX, WHICH SERVE TO STORE FOOD FOR THE WINTER AND AS A NURSERY FOR YOUNG LARVAE.

IN BEE SOCIETY, EACH INDIVIDUAL HAS A TASK TO PERFORM. THE QUEEN BEE, WHO IS THE LARGEST OF ALL, LAYS EGGS AND DIRECTS THE WORK. THE WORKERS ARE HER DAUGHTERS; THEY CLEAN AND PROTECT THE HIVE, CARE FOR THE QUEEN AND LARVAE, AND PROVIDE FOOD COLLECTION. THE DRONES ARE THE MALES AND HAVE THE SOLE TASK OF FERTILIZING THE QUEEN BEE.

1 queen

EACH HIVE CONSISTS OF ONE QUEEN THAT CAN LAY 2,500 EGGS A DAY, 10,000 TO 60,000 WORKER BEES, AND SEVERAL DOZEN DRONES.

110 lb

EACH BEEHIVE PRODUCES AN AVERAGE OF 44 TO 110 LB (20 TO 50 KG) OF HONEY IN A YEAR. TO PRODUCE ONE POT OF HONEY, NECTAR AND POLLEN FROM ABOUT 2 MILLION FLOWERS ARE NEEDED.

20,000

THERE ARE MORE THAN 20,000 SPECIES OF BEES ON EARTH. THEY LIVE ALL OVER THE WORLD, WITH THE EXCEPTION OF ANTARCTICA.

70 percent

DOMESTIC AND WILD BEES ARE RESPONSIBLE FOR ABOUT 70 PERCENT OF THE POLLINATION OF ALL LIVING PLANT SPECIES ON THE PLANET.

WORKER BEE

THIS IS A FEMALE THAT IS INFERTILE BECAUSE OF A PARTICULAR DIET AND BECAUSE OF THE INHIBITORY PHEROMONES EMITTED BY THE QUEEN.

BUTTERFLIES AND MOTHS

Both are fascinating winged insects of the Lepidoptera order.

However, their lifestyles are different: butterflies fly during the day, while moths are more active at night. Butterflies rest by closing their wings book-like over their backs, while most moths keep them closed horizontally.

The largest MOTH

THE HERCULES MOTH HAS WINGS THAT REACH A WIDTH OF NEARLY 12 IN (30 CM).

ADULT BUTTERFLY

EGGS

CATERPILLARS

CATERPILLARS EAT NONSTOP, AND IN JUST TWO WEEKS THEY CAN GROW UP TO 3,000 TIMES THEIR ORIGINAL SIZE.

LIFE CYCLE OF A BUTTERFLY

THE LIFE OF A BUTTERFLY IS MARKED IN FOUR STAGES: EGG, CATERPILLAR, PUPA, AND ADULT BUTTERFLY. THE ADULT LIFE IS SHORT, FROM A COUPLE OF DAYS TO A FEW WEEKS, BUT THERE IS NO SHORTAGE OF MUCH LONGER-LIVED TYPES, SUCH AS THE *VANESSA ANTIOPIA*, WHICH LIVES ALMOST AN ENTIRE YEAR.

CATERPILLAR

PUPA (OR CHRYSALIS)

The PUPA

AT THIS STAGE THE LARVA CREATES A COCOON AROUND ITSELF WITHIN WHICH THE TRANSFORMATION INTO A BUTTERFLY TAKES PLACE.

Different ANTENNAS

LIKE ALL INSECTS, THEY "SNIFF" WITH THEIR ANTENNAS, WHICH GENERALLY IN BUTTERFLIES ARE CLUB-SHAPED WITH A BALL AT THE END, WHILE IN MOTHS THEY ARE FEATHERY, SAW-SHAPED, OR TAPERED.

What COLORS!

THE WINGS OF BUTTERFLIES CAN BE BRIGHT AND MULTICOLORED. THE PATTERNS AND COLORS DEPEND ON THE ARRANGEMENT OF THE THOUSANDS OF TINY SCALES THAT COVER THEM.

The largest BUTTERFLY

THE FEMALE QUEEN ALEXANDRA BUTTERFLY IS THE LARGEST, THANKS TO A WINGSPAN OF MORE THAN 9.8 IN (25 CM).

Thanks to the MOON

MOTHS FIND THEIR WAY AT NIGHT BY MOONLIGHT. HOWEVER, THIS MEANS THAT THEY CAN ALSO BE ATTRACTED TO ARTIFICIAL LIGHTS, RISKING LOSING THEIR ORIENTATION.

With a STRAW

BUTTERFLIES AND MOTHS FEED ON LIQUID FOOD, WHICH THEY SUCK UP WITH A LONG STRAW-LIKE TONGUE CALLED A SPIROTROMBA. THEY USUALLY SUCK NECTAR FROM FLOWERS, BUT SOME HAVE QUESTIONABLE TASTE AND PREFER TO DRINK TEARS, BLOOD, AND DECAYING LIQUIDS.

MONARCH BUTTERFLY

THE MONARCH IS A MIGRATORY BUTTERFLY, CAPABLE OF FLYING INCREDIBLE DISTANCES. IT WAS DISCOVERED, FOR EXAMPLE, THAT ONE INDIVIDUAL OF THIS SPECIES TRAVELED 1,312 MILES (2,112 KM) IN 46 DAYS.

GIANT ANIMALS

The TALLEST

GIRAFFES ARE DEFINITELY THE TALLEST ANIMALS ON EARTH. AN ADULT MALE REACHES ALMOST 19.6 FT (6 M) IN HEIGHT, OF WHICH 7.8 FT (2.4 M) IS THE VERY LONG NECK ALONE.

By weight, height, or length, some animals are truly enormous.

Even compared to similar species, and even among the "little" species, you can find extra large specimens. These titanic creatures remind us of the enormous biodiversity of our planet and the importance of conserving its many natural habitats.

The LARGEST in the world

WITH A LONG, SLENDER BODY REACHING A LENGTH OF 98 FT (30 M), THE BLUE WHALE IS BY FAR THE LARGEST KNOWN ANIMAL.

A GIANT among the LITTLE ONES

THE GIANT SNAIL, AN AFRICAN MOLLUSK, HAS A SHELL EXCEEDING 7.87 IN (20 CM) IN LENGTH AND WEIGHS 2.2 LB (1 KG).

What EYES!

THE LARGEST COLOSSAL SQUID *(MESONYCHOTEUTHIS HAMILTONI)* EVER DOCUMENTED WAS 46 FT (14 M) LONG AND HAD EYES 19.7 IN (50 CM) IN DIAMETER, THE LARGEST EYES IN THE WORLD.

LARGE FLYING FOX

AMONG BATS, THE LARGEST SPECIES IS THE MALAYAN FLYING FOX, WHICH MEASURES NEARLY 6.5 FT (2 M) WHEN IT SPREADS ITS WINGS. THESE BATS ARE VALUABLE POLLINATORS, FEEDING ON FRUIT AND DISPERSING SEEDS.

Among the BIRDS

THE GIANT AMONG PRESENT-DAY BIRDS IS THE OSTRICH. A MALE CAN MEASURE ABOUT 9 FT (2.75 M) IN HEIGHT AND CAN WEIGH UP TO 344 LB (156 KG). SUCH A LARGE BIRD CANNOT FLY, BUT IT RUNS AT A SPEED OF UP TO 43.5 MILES PER HOUR (70 KM/H) WHILE SPRINTING.

Among the AMPHIBIANS

THE CHINESE GIANT SALAMANDER IS THE LARGEST AMPHIBIAN IN THE WORLD, REACHING A LENGTH OF 6 FT (1.8 M). THESE ANIMALS HAVE EXISTED FOR MILLIONS OF YEARS AND HAVE REMAINED UNCHANGED OVER TIME.

Among the FISH

THE WHALE SHARK IS UNDOUBTEDLY THE LARGEST FISH ON EARTH, MEASURING 61.6 FT (19 M) IN LENGTH.

AFRICAN ELEPHANT

THIS IS THE LARGEST LAND ANIMAL. THE BIGGEST MALES CAN REACH A HEIGHT AT THE SHOULDER OF UP TO 13 FT (4 M).

Among the REPTILES

THE GREEN ANACONDA IS THE WORLD'S HEAVIEST SNAKE AS WELL AS ONE OF THE LONGEST, REACHING A LENGTH OF 26.2 FT (8 M).

SLOW AND FAST ANIMALS

Life, as we know, can be approached at various speeds.

There are animals that move as fast as lightning, while others are content to move only a few feet per minute. Contrary to appearances, the latter are proof that even slowness can have advantages.

SLOTH

THE SLOTH IS THE QUINTESSENTIAL SYMBOL OF ANIMAL SLOWNESS. IT SPENDS THE DAY HANGING FROM A TREE BRANCH, FROM WHICH IT DESCENDS ONLY ONCE A WEEK–TO POOP!

No HURRY!

MANATEES, ALSO CALLED SEA COWS, ARE CALM IN THEIR MOVEMENTS. IN FACT, THEY SWIM PEACEFULLY AT THE SPEED OF 1.8 TO 3.1 MILES PER HOUR (3-5 KM/H).

The SLOWEST Fish

THE DWARF SEAHORSE MOVES 5 FT (1.5 M) IN AN HOUR AND IS THE SLOWEST FISH IN THE WORLD. TO ESCAPE PREDATORS, INSTEAD OF SWIMMING AWAY, IT REMAINS MOTIONLESS AND CAMOUFLAGES ITSELF.

Gliding CALMLY

THOSE WITH ONLY ONE FOOT CAN HARDLY MOVE FAST. THE COMMON SNAIL SLIDES ITS MUSCULAR LOCOMOTOR ORGAN OVER ITS MUCUS TO REDUCE FRICTION BUT STILL ADVANCES ONLY 9.8 FT (3 M) PER HOUR, TAKING TWO WEEKS TO TRAVEL A KILOMETER.

CHEETAH

THE WORLD CHAMPION AMONG SPRINTERS IS THE CHEETAH. IT CAN REACH A TOP SPEED OF ALMOST 70 MILES PER HOUR (112 KM/H), ALTHOUGH IT CANNOT MAINTAIN IT FOR MORE THAN 1,312 FT (400 M).

NOSEDIVE!

THE PEREGRINE FALCON STRIKES ITS PREY IN FLIGHT, SWOOPING DOWN AT THE INSANE SPEED OF 112 MILES PER HOUR (180 KM/H), WITH A LITTLE HELP FROM GRAVITY.

BUG or helicopter?

WITH 20 BEATS PER SECOND OF ITS LONG MEMBRANOUS WINGS, THE DRAGONFLY HURTLES THROUGH THE AIR AT AN INCREDIBLE SPEED OF 31 MILES PER HOUR (50 KM/H).

SPEED & endurance

THE WHITE-THROATED NEEDLETAIL SWIFT IS UNBEATABLE IN HORIZONTAL FLIGHT. ACCORDING TO SCIENTISTS, IT CAN REACH MORE THAN 105 MILES PER HOUR (170 KM/H) DURING LONG ANNUAL MIGRATIONS.

The FASTEST among the waves

AT SEA, THE RECORD FOR THE FASTEST ANIMAL IS HELD BY THE PACIFIC SAILFISH. IT HAS A SWIMMING SPEED OF UP TO 62 MILES PER HOUR (100 KM/H)!

COURTSHIP

In the animal world, many animal species resort to courtship rituals—sometimes very peculiar ones!

Courtship is a strategy adopted mainly by male animals to impress females and get chosen as the father of their children. The tactics used to draw attention to themselves can be really strange.

DO-RE-MI

THERE ARE SINGING CHAMPIONS AMONG HUMPBACK WHALES: MALES PERFORM MELODIES LASTING 20 MINUTES THAT ARE COMPARED BY SCIENTISTS TO CLASSICAL MUSIC. THE SOUND PROPAGATES THROUGH THE WATER, COVERING DISTANCES OF UP TO 1,864 MILES (3,000 KM).

SKILLED decorators

GARDEN BIRDS DEMONSTRATE THEIR NEST-BUILDING SKILLS BY CREATING STRANGE U-SHAPED TUNNELS WITH TWIGS AND ADORNED WITH COLORFUL OBJECTS, PREFERABLY BLUE ONES.

How ROMANTIC!

MALES OF *TILIQUA RUGOSA*, AN AUSTRALIAN REPTILE, ARE AMONG THE MOST TENDER SUITORS; WHEN THEY MEET A FEMALE, THEY WALK NEXT TO HER, "CUDDLING" HER FROM TIME TO TIME WITH GENTLE NUDGES WITH THEIR SNOUT. THIS ROMANTIC WALK CAN LAST UP TO TWO MONTHS.

FIREFLIES

FIREFLIES (LAMPYRIDAE) ATTRACT EACH OTHER BY SENDING OUT LIGHT SIGNALS. THEIR FLASHES CAN BE SEEN AS FAR AS 50 FEET (15 M) AWAY.

HARD heads

SOME SPECIES RESORT TO TESTS OF STRENGTH. MALE IBEX *(CAPRA IBEX)* FIGHT BY SLAMMING THEIR MASSIVE HORNS, NEARLY 3 FT (1 M) LONG AND WEIGHING 8.8 LB (4 KG), AGAINST EACH OTHER. THEIR HORNS ARE VERY STRONG AND ELASTIC.

A little GIFT

AMONG ADÉLIE PENGUINS *(PYGOSCELIS ADELIAE)* IT IS CUSTOMARY FOR MALES TO SEARCH THE BEACHES FOR SMOOTH PEBBLES THAT THEY BRING AS GIFTS TO FEMALES. IF APPRECIATED, THEY WILL BE USED FOR NESTING.

PEACOCK

TO IMPRESS THE FEMALE, THE MALE PEACOCK RAISES ITS LONG, BEAUTIFUL FEATHERS, ARRANGING THEM AS IF THEY WERE A FAN.

HIBERNATION

Some animals resort to hibernation, or deep sleep, to survive cold, dark winters when there is little food available.

Having found a safe place, they indulge in a period of inactivity in an almost unconscious state, waiting for the warm season. It also happens when it gets too hot; in this case it is called estivation, and it allows animals to survive the extreme temperatures and lack of food and water.

Cold BLOOD

SNAKES AND LIZARDS ALSO SEEK SHELTER DURING THE COLD SEASON. IN COLD-BLOODED ANIMALS THIS WINTER REST IS CALLED BRUMATION.

Useful FLAB

TO PREPARE FOR THE LONG PERIOD WHEN THEY WILL NEITHER EAT NOR BE ABLE TO DRINK, ANIMALS EAT A LOT, AND BY THE END OF SUMMER THEY CAN DOUBLE THEIR WEIGHT.

BEARS

IN WINTER, BEARS FALL INTO A DEEP SLEEP FROM WHICH THEY AWAKEN WITH SOME FREQUENCY. FEMALES AT THIS TIME GIVE BIRTH AND NURSE THEIR YOUNG IN THE SHELTER OF THE WINTER DEN.

7 months

THE AMOUNT OF TIME A WOOD FROG CAN SURVIVE BEING FROZEN, THANKS TO A SUBSTANCE IN ITS BLOOD. ITS HEART STOPS BEATING, AND ITS BLOOD STOPS FLOWING. WHEN THE TIME IS RIGHT, IT THAWS OUT.

A slow BEAT

DURING HIBERNATION AN ANIMAL´S HEARTBEAT DECELERATES AND SO DOES ITS METABOLISM.

6 months

THE MADAGASCAR FAT-TAILED DWARF LEMUR IS THE ONLY KNOWN PRIMATE THAT SPENDS THE SIX DRY WINTER MONTHS SLEEPING INSIDE A HOLE IN A TREE, SURVIVING OFF OF THE FAT RESERVES IT HAS STORED IN ITS TAIL.

DORMOUSE

WITH THE ARRIVAL OF COLD AUTUMN DAYS, DORMICE BECOME TOTALLY INACTIVE TO CONSERVE ENERGY. HEART RATE AND RESPIRATION SLOW DOWN, AND BODY TEMPERATURE DECREASES.

SHARKS AND RAYS

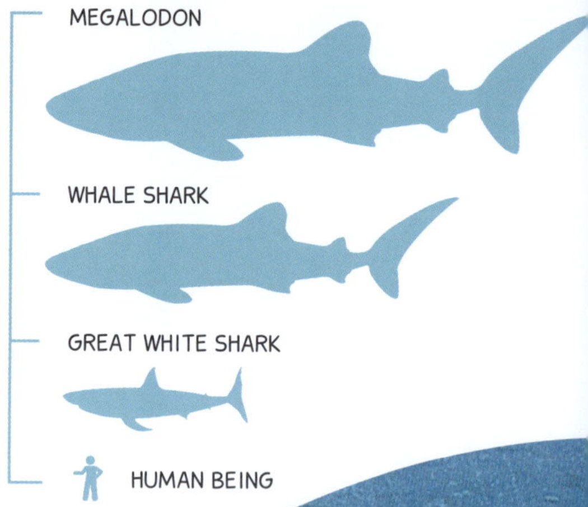

They make up a subgroup of fish with the difficult scientific name of Chondrichthyes.

Unlike most fish, they have a skeleton made of cartilage, a substance that is lighter and more elastic than bone. Their skin is not covered with scales like other fish, but with lots of very hard-tipped denticles.

TEETH

THE MOST TERRIFYING FEATURE OF SHARKS IS THEIR NUMEROUS SHARP, POINTED TEETH, WHICH ARE ARRANGED IN MULTIPLE ROWS WITHIN THE JAW. THE SHARK USES ONLY THE ONES IN THE FIRST ROW, AND THE OTHERS MOVE FORWARD AS THEY REPLACE WORN-OUT ONES.

7.09 in

THE LENGTH OF THE LARGEST TOOTH OF A SHARK FOSSIL EVER FOUND-THE MEGALODON. THIS SUGGESTS THAT THE ANCIENT FISH WAS 56 FT (17 M) LONG: LARGER THAN A BUS!

The LARGEST...

...AT 46 FT (14 M), IS THE WHALE SHARK. IT FEEDS ONLY ON TINY ORGANISMS AND IS TOTALLY HARMLESS.

400 MILION...

...YEARS AGO, THE FIRST SHARKS LIVED!

GREAT WHITE SHARK

IT IS FOUND IN THE COASTAL WATERS OF ALL MAJOR OCEANS. IT HAS A LENGTH OF 15 TO 16 FT (4.6 TO 4.9 M) FOR THE FEMALE AND 11 TO 13 FT (3.4 TO 4 M) FOR THE MALE. ITS WEIGHT VARIES FROM 1,499 TO 2,425 LB (680-1,100 KG), AND IT CAN REACH A SPEED OF 34.7 MILES PER HOUR (56 KM/H). ITS JUMPS CAN REACH 14.7 FT (4.5 M) ABOVE SEA LEVEL.

135

THE NUMBER OF PUPS A FEMALE BLUE SHARK CAN GIVE BIRTH TO AT ONE TIME.

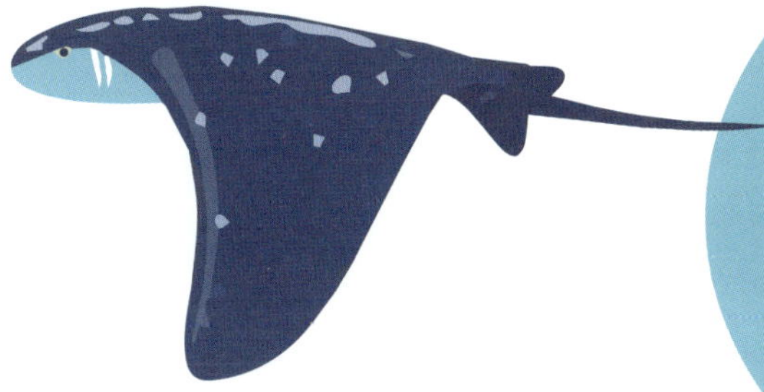

More than 23 FT

THE WIDTH THAT THE LARGEST MANTA RAY CAN REACH.

The RAYS

RAYS ARE CLOSE RELATIVES OF SHARKS. HOWEVER, THEIR BODIES ARE FLATTENED, AND THEIR PECTORAL FINS ARE JOINED TO THE SIDES OF THEIR HEADS TO FORM "WINGS" THAT MOVE IN THE WATER AS THEY SWIM. MANY GLIDE ALONG THE SEABED FEEDING ON CRUSTACEANS, MOLLUSKS, AND SMALL FISH HIDDEN IN THE SAND.

SHORTFIN MAKO

The FASTEST

THE MAKO SHARK REACHES 50 MPH (80 KM/H). SHARKS ARE GOOD SWIMMERS. THEY MOVE PROPELLED BY THEIR TAILS, WHICH SWING FROM SIDE TO SIDE. THE PECTORAL FINS CONTROL DIRECTION, WHILE THE DORSAL FIN KEEPS THE BODY BALANCED. INSTEAD OF A SWIM BLADDER THEY HAVE A VERY LARGE LIVER FILLED WITH OIL, WHICH FACILITATES BUOYANCY.

SIXTH SENSE

IN ADDITION TO AN EXCELLENT SENSE OF SMELL AND GOOD EYESIGHT, SHARKS HAVE AN EXTRA SENSE WITH WHICH THEY CAN DETECT TINY ELECTROMAGNETIC FIELDS. THEY USE IT TO FIND BURIED FOOD OR TO SEARCH FOR PREY IN DARK OR MURKY WATER. FOR THIS THEY HAVE SPECIAL ORGANS, CALLED AMPULLAE OF LORENZINI, PLACED NEAR THE NOSE, EYES, AND MOUTH.

BIRDS OF PREY

There are two types of raptors: those that are diurnal, or active during the day, and those that are nocturnal, or active at dusk and when it's dark.

Typically, their eyesight is four times sharper than ours, and they have super hearing.

Nocturnes

Elf OWL

IT IS ONE OF THE SMALLEST OWLS IN THE WORLD, AT 5.7 IN (14.5 CM) IN LENGTH AND 1.2-1.5 OZ (36-44 G) IN WEIGHT.

Ssssh

THE BARN OWL IS KNOWN TO HAVE THE QUIETEST FLIGHT AMONG ALL BIRDS.

1500

THE NUMBER OF SMALL RODENTS, MAINLY LEMMINGS, THAT A SNOWY OWL CAN HUNT IN A YEAR.

ALWAYS on the alert!

NIGHT RAPTORS CAN SEE EVERYWHERE WITHOUT HAVING TO MOVE THEIR EYES. THANKS TO THEIR SPECIAL VERY FLEXIBLE NECK, THEY ARE ABLE TO ROTATE THEIR HEADS 270 DEGREES, OR THREE-QUARTERS OF A FULL TURN.

EAGLE OWL

IT IS THE LARGEST OWL SPECIES, WITH A WINGSPAN OF 5.2 TO 6.5 FT (1.60 TO 2.0 M). IT SPENDS MOST OF ITS LIFE NEAR ITS NEST.

Daytime

BALD EAGLE

IT HAS BEEN THE SYMBOL OF THE UNITED STATES SINCE 1782. ITS REMARKABLE WINGSPAN CAN REACH UP TO 6.5 FT (2 M)!

GIANT nest

ONE OF THE WORLD'S LARGEST NESTS WAS FOUND IN FLORIDA AND WAS BUILT BY A BALD EAGLE: IT WAS NEARLY 20 FT BY 10 FT (6 M BY 3 M).

What a VIEW!

IT IS POSSIBLE FOR VULTURES TO SPOT THE CARCASS OF A DEAD ANIMAL MORE THAN 3 MILES (5 KM) AWAY WHILE CIRCLING IN THE AIR.

FALCONRY

FALCONRY IS A HUNTING PRACTICE THAT ORIGINATED MORE THAN 10,000 YEARS AGO FROM THE COLLABORATION BETWEEN HUMANS AND TRAINED FALCONS.

Black-thighed FALCONET

THE SIZE OF RAPTORS VARIES WIDELY. SOME ARE REALLY SMALL, SUCH AS THE BLACK-THIGHED FLACONET, WHICH IS ONLY 5-6 IN (14-16 CM) LONG.

Andes CONDOR

THIS ENDANGERED SPECIES IS CONSIDERED THE LARGEST BIRD OF PREY, WITH A WINGSPAN OF MORE THAN 9.8 FT (3 M). IT CAN FLY UP TO AN ALTITUDE OF 18,000 FT (5,500 M).

13,670 miles

THIS IS THE INCREDIBLE DISTANCE THE AMUR FALCON CAN TRAVEL AS IT MIGRATES FROM SIBERIA TO SOUTH AFRICA.

WADING BIRDS

They are often found in shallow water, balancing on long, thin, stilt-like legs.

Their toes are also thin, making it easier to walk without slipping on the slimy bottom of bodies of water.

JACANA

THE JACANA HAS UNIQUELY DISPROPORTIONATE TOES! BY WIDENING THEM, IT CAN WALK SAFELY, EVEN ON FLOATING AQUATIC PLANTS.

A lover of CLEANLINESS

A BEACH FREQUENTED BY THE LITTLE PLOVER IS DEFINITELY CLEAN. IN FACT, THIS LITTLE BIRD LIVES ONLY IN POLLUTION-FREE AREAS IN A NATURAL STATE. IT RUNS BACK AND FORTH ALONG THE BEACH, DIPPING ITS BEAK IN THE MUD FROM TIME TO TIME TO LOOK FOR FOOD.

A challenging NECK

GREY HERONS HAVE SUCH A LONG NECK THAT THEY HAVE TO KEEP IT BENT EVEN WHEN FLYING. TRIGGERING IT LIKE A SPRING, THEY SPEAR FISH WITH THE LONG POINTED BEAK, WHICH THEY USE AS A HARPOON.

COMMON CRANE

AT 3.9 FT (1.20 M) TALL, THE WHOOPING CRANE *(GRUS GRUS)* IS THE LARGEST BIRD CAPABLE OF FLIGHT. IT IS FAMOUS FOR ITS MIGRATIONS OF THOUSANDS OF MILES, WHICH IT UNDERTAKES IN FLOCKS OF UP TO 1,000 INDIVIDUALS, ARRANGING THEMSELVES IN FLIGHT IN THE CLASSIC V SHAPE.

Head DOWN!

THE FLAMINGO'S LARGE BLACK BEAK HAS A STRANGE SHAPE, WITH ITS CURVED TIP SLOPING DOWNWARD. ITS BEAK IS USED TO COLLECT WATER. INSIDE, LAMELLAE ACT AS FILTERS BY TRAPPING THE SMALL ORGANISMS THAT ARE ITS MEAL.

FOOD

WADING BIRDS GENERALLY EAT FISH, CRUSTACEANS, AND MOLLUSKS, BUT OFTEN ALSO PREY FOUND ON LAND, SUCH AS INSECTS, AMPHIBIANS, AND SMALL REPTILES.

Delicate FEATHERS

STANDING 3.28 FT (1 M) TALL, THE GREAT WHITE EGRET IS LARGE ENOUGH THAT IT CAN'T GO UNNOTICED. ITS PLUMAGE, SNOW WHITE AND VERY DELICATE, WAS ONCE USED AS A HAT ORNAMENT.

FLAMINGO

THE DELICATE PINKISH COLOR OF FLAMINGOS COMES FROM WHAT THEY EAT, WHICH IS PREDOMINANTLY SMALL CRUSTACEANS CONTAINING A RED-ORANGE PIGMENT.

PARROTS AND TOUCANS

They are among the most beautiful and colorful birds on Earth.

Although there is no kinship between them, they have something in common: They are both good tree climbers and are distinguished by their intelligence and sociability.

Well-protected EGGS

TO MAKE THEIR NESTS, TOUCANS CHOOSE A HOLE IN THE TRUNK OF A TREE AND LAY TWO TO FOUR EGGS THERE, WHICH ARE TAKEN CARE OF IN TURN BY THE PARENTS FOR 20 DAYS.

A little CLUMSY!

ALTHOUGH LIGHT, ITS HUGE BEAK UNBALANCES THE TOUCAN WHILE FLYING, WHICH RESULTS IN A SLOW AND CLUMSY FLIGHT. IN ADDITION, THE WINGS ARE SMALL AND ARE USED TO COVER ONLY SHORT DISTANCES. THEREFORE, TOUCANS SPEND MORE TIME HOPPING FROM TREE TO TREE THAN FLYING.

An all-around BEAK

ALL TOUCANS HAVE A LARGE BEAK, LIGHTER THAN IT LOOKS, WHICH THEY USE LIKE TONGS TO PICK UP FOOD. THANKS TO THE BEAK'S SERRATED EDGE, THE TOUCAN PEELS THE FLESHY FRUITS OF THE FOREST WITH INCREDIBLE DEXTERITY.

What a NOISE!

TOUCANS ARE AMONG THE NOISIEST BIRDS IN THE WORLD, AND THEIR VOICES CAN BE QUITE UNPLEASANT. IN FACT, THEY SEEM TO BARK, GROWL, AND BRAY! THEY EVEN MAKE NOISE BY DRUMMING WITH THEIR BEAKS.

PARROT to whom?

"PARROT" IS A GENERIC WORD FOR SEVERAL SPECIES GENERALLY ENDOWED WITH A LARGE, STURDY, POINTED BEAK; BRIGHT COLORS; AND AN INNATE KNACK FOR IMITATING SOUNDS, INCLUDING THE HUMAN VOICE.

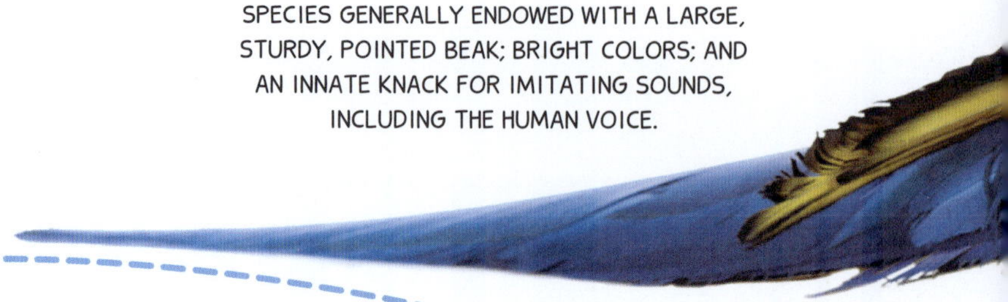

Yummy SEEDS

THE DIET OF PARROTS IS QUITE VARIED: IN ADDITION TO FRUITS, VEGETABLES, AND VARIOUS SEEDS, THEY CAN ALSO EAT SMALL INVERTEBRATES, SUCH AS INSECTS. HOWEVER, SEEDS AND DRIED FRUITS ARE THEIR FAVORITE FOODS.

Great FRIENDS

PARROTS PREFER TO LIVE WITH THEIR PEERS, AND SOME SPECIES EVEN STARVE THEMSELVES TO DEATH IF LEFT ALONE.

BLAH, BLAH, BLAH

WE KNOW THE CHATTERING ABILITY OF PARROTS, BUT ONE EXCEEDED EXPECTATIONS: A CALIFORNIA WOMAN'S WAVY PARAKEET KNEW AS MANY AS 1,728 WORDS.

86 years old

THE VENERABLE AGE ATTAINED BY A PINK COCKATOO AT A CHICAGO ZOO. PARROTS CAN HAVE A SURPRISINGLY LONG LIFE SPAN, COMPARABLE TO THAT OF HUMANS!

About 350

THE KNOWN SPECIES OF PARROTS; OF THESE, MOST LIVE IN TROPICAL AND SUBTROPICAL REGIONS.

BLUE MACAW

IT IS A QUIET, DOCILE, AND GREGARIOUS BIRD THAT IS ALSO A GOOD MIMIC. IT HAS VERY FEW ENEMIES IN THE WILD (IF YOU EXCLUDE HUMANS, WHO ARE DESTROYING ITS HABITATS).

PENGUINS

Penguins are birds; however, they are unable to fly.

On land they walk somewhat awkwardly, while they are very skilled in swimming. Their bodies are hydrodynamic, and their wings have become fins; their plumage is especially thick and waterproof so that they glide through water better.

37 MILLION years ago

COLOSSAL PENGUINS EXISTED. THEY WERE 6.5 FT (2 M) TALL AND WEIGHED 330.7 LB (150 KG).

Some PRIVACY

WHILE MOST PENGUINS NEST IN COLONIES, NEW ZEALAND'S YELLOW-EYED PENGUINS *(MEGADYPTES ANTIPODES)* PREFER A SECLUDED LIFE IN PAIRS AND BUILD THEIR NESTS IN THE FOREST, AS FAR AS .6 MILE (1 KM) AWAY FROM THE COAST.

What a VOICE!

TO BE ABLE TO COMMUNICATE WITH OTHER MEMBERS OF THE COLONY, PENGUINS MAKE GREAT USE OF THEIR VOICES. THE AFRICAN PENGUIN PRODUCES A CRY REMINISCENT OF A DONKEY'S BRAYING, WHICH HAS EARNED IT THE NICKNAME "DONKEY."

FOREVER

PENGUINS ARE FAITHFUL COMPANIONS. EACH BREEDING SEASON ADÉLIE PENGUINS RETURN TO THE SAME PLACE TO MEET THE SAME PARTNER, WITH WHOM THEY COLLECT STONES TO BUILD THE NEST.

LARGE and small

BETWEEN SPECIES, SIZE CAN VARY GREATLY, RANGING FROM THE BLUE PENGUIN AT A HEIGHT OF 11.81 IN (30 CM) TO THE EMPEROR PENGUIN, THE WORLD'S LARGEST, AT A HEIGHT OF 51.18 IN (130 CM).

Brrrr

TO WITHSTAND TEMPERATURES THAT CAN PLUMMET TO -104°F (-40°C), EMPEROR PENGUINS HAVE THE THICKEST PLUMAGE OF ANY BIRD. THERE ARE ABOUT 80 FEATHERS ON A SKIN AREA OF JUST 0.98 IN^2 (2.5 CM^2).

BLACK and WHITE

MANY PREDATORS HIDE IN THE OCEANS, BUT THE PENGUINS' COLORATION HELPS THEM SURVIVE: WHEN VIEWED FROM ABOVE, THE BLACK OF THEIR BACKS CAMOUFLAGES THEM IN THE DARK SEABED, WHILE WHEN VIEWED FROM BELOW, THE WHITE OF THEIR BELLIES MAKES THEM BLEND IN WITH THE SUNLIT SURFACE.

All to the SOUTH!

ALL 18 SPECIES OF PENGUINS LIVE IN THE SOUTHERN HEMISPHERE. THEY ARE FOUND IN ANTARCTICA AND ON SUBANTARCTIC ISLANDS AS WELL AS IN NEW ZEALAND, AUSTRALIA, SOUTH AMERICA, AFRICA, AND EVEN THE GALAPAGOS ISLANDS.

KING PENGUIN

LIKE MANY OTHER SPECIES, KING PENGUINS LIVE IN HUGE COLONIES CONSISTING OF HUNDREDS OF INDIVIDUALS.

CAMOUFLAGED ANIMALS

Deceiving those who are watching you may seem like a game, but in nature it can mean the difference between life and death.

This art of deception is called mimicry, and it comes in many forms, among both prey and predators. Imitation may involve not only appearance, but also sounds, smells, or behaviors.

Master of IMITATION

THE MIMIC OCTOPUS MANAGES TO IMITATE AS MANY AS 15 ANIMALS BY STRETCHING, WRITHING, AND CHANGING COLOR. IT CAN IMITATE A SEA SNAKE, A JELLYFISH, A LIONFISH, A CRAB, AND MORE...

What a SCARE!

MANY BUTTERFLIES HAVE TWO LARGE CIRCULAR SPOTS ON THEIR WINGS THAT RESEMBLE THE EYES OF MUCH LARGER ANIMALS, SUCH AS OWLS. BY PUTTING THEM ON DISPLAY, THE BUTTERFLY IS ABLE TO FOOL AND SCARE OFF PREDATORS!

A brilliant DISGUISE

BECAUSE BEES AND WASPS KNOW HOW TO DEFEND THEMSELVES WITH THEIR STING, THEY ARE USUALLY LEFT ALONE BY PREDATORS. SOME INSECTS RELATED TO FLIES MIMIC THEIR YELLOW AND BLACK COLORS TO IMITATE THEM AND NOT BE ATTACKED.

Every trick IS VALID!

WHEN IT COMES OUT OF THE EGG, THE SWALLOWTAIL BUTTERFLY CATERPILLAR IS SMALL AND BROWN WITH WHITE STRIPES. IN SHORT, IT LOOKS LIKE BIRD POOP!

ENGINEERING method

SOME ANIMALS NOT NATURALLY ENDOWED WITH CAMOUFLAGE ARE ABLE TO USE CAMOUFLAGE BY COVERING THEMSELVES WITH WHAT THEY FIND LYING AROUND. THE HERMIT CRAB, FOR EXAMPLE, OCCUPIES AN EMPTY SHELL AND COVERS IT WITH SPONGES AND SEA ANEMONES TO HIDE ON THE SEAFLOOR.

Spider CHEATERS!

THERE ARE MORE THAN 300 SPECIES OF SPIDERS CAPABLE OF IMITATING THE APPEARANCE OF ANTS. WITH THIS TRICK THEY NOT ONLY APPROACH PREY MORE EASILY, BUT ALSO AVOID BEING CAUGHT THEMSELVES BECAUSE OTHER PREDATORS KNOW THE AGGRESSIVENESS OF THE HARDWORKING LITTLE ANTS.

STICK insect

DESPITE ITS 11.8 IN (30 CM) LENGTH, IT IS NOT EASY TO SPOT THE STICK INSECT BECAUSE IT LOOKS EXACTLY LIKE A TWIG!

LEAF INSECT

INCREDIBLY, IT RESEMBLES A LEAF. EVEN ITS EGGS ADOPT A CAMOUFLAGE MECHANISM BECAUSE OF THEIR COMPLETELY IDENTICAL APPEARANCE TO SMALL SEEDS.

VENOMOUS ANIMALS

Many animals produce substances that are more or less lethal.

Depending on the species, venomous substances can be used in completely different ways on an animal's attackers or prey. Often they are injected by a bite or sting; in other cases just a touch is enough to absorb the venom.

The most POISONOUS

THE WORLD'S MOST VENOMOUS SNAKE IS BELIEVED TO BE THE TAIPAN, CAPABLE OF INJECTING ENOUGH VENOM IN A SINGLE DOSE TO KILL 200,000 MICE!

MEDICINES?

MIXTURES OF ANIMAL TOXINS ARE OFTEN STUDIED AS PAINKILLERS AND TO TREAT MAJOR HUMAN DISEASES.

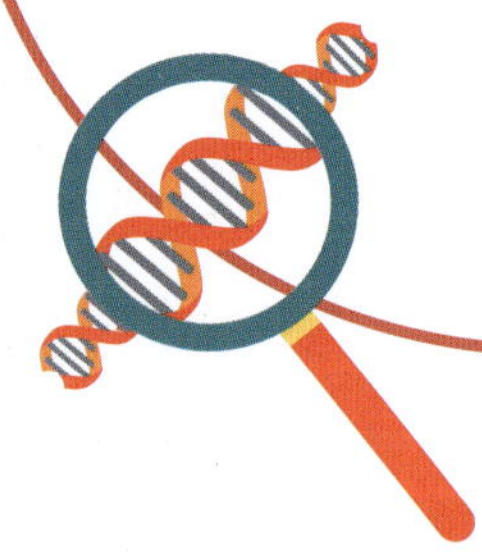

A DANGEROUS fish

SOME ORGANS OF THE PUFFERFISH CONTAIN TOXINS THAT AFFECT THE NERVOUS SYSTEM AND ARE DANGEROUS TO HUMANS. HOWEVER, THE MEAT OF SOME SPECIES IS EATEN, BUT ONLY WHEN COOKED BY AN EXPERIENCED AND LICENSED CHEF.

No ANTIDOTE!

THE TINY BLUE-RINGED OCTOPUS CAN POISON 25 ADULTS IN A MATTER OF MINUTES, LEAVING THEM NO ESCAPE!

DEADLY Tentacles

JELLYFISH HAVE A STINGING LIQUID IN THEIR TENTACLES THAT THEY CAN INJECT INTO THE SKIN EVEN IF YOU JUST BRUSH AGAINST THEM. MANY SPECIES, INCLUDING THE BOX JELLYFISH, ARE DEADLY.

A SECRET!

THE FRIENDLY PLATYPUS HIDES A SECRET IN ITS HIND LEG SPUR. IN MALE-TO-MALE FIGHTS A PLATYPUS CAN WEAKEN ITS COMPETITOR BY INJECTING A POISON AND CAUSING HIM SEVERE PAIN THAT LASTS FOR DAYS.

DANGEROUS spiders!

AMONG THE MOST VENOMOUS IS THE BURROWING SPIDER, WHICH, WITH FANGS ALMOST 0.39 IN (1 CM) LONG, CAUSES EXTREMELY PAINFUL BITES.

THE BANANA SPIDER HAS VENOM SEVEN TIMES MORE POWERFUL THAN THE MORE FAMOUS BLACK WIDOW. JUST A FEW DROPS ARE ENOUGH TO MAKE VICTIMS VERY ILL.

POISON DART FROG

ITS BRIGHT COLORS LET PREDATORS KNOW THAT THE SMALL FROG IS NOT A SUITABLE MEAL! IN FACT, ITS VENOM IS STORED IN THE SKIN AND AFFECTS ANYONE WHO TOUCHES OR EATS IT.

PARASITES

Some animals have found a way to survive at another's expense: They are the parasites.

The two species involved are in a perpetual struggle, as one tries hard to take advantage of the situation, while the other has to implement a strategy in order to not succumb.

ZOMBIE bugs

IT SOUNDS LIKE A HORROR STORY! THE OPHIOCORDYCEPS FUNGI IS ABLE TO TAKE CONTROL OF THE MUSCLES AND NERVOUS SYSTEM OF CREATURES LIKE ANTS AND CATERPILLARS IN ORDER TO BE TRANSPORTED TO AN IDEAL PLACE FOR THE DISPERSAL OF ITS SPORES.

Help, A VAMPIRE!

THE VAMPIRE BAT, WHICH LIVES IN SOUTH AMERICA, FEEDS ON THE BLOOD OF THE VICTIMS IT BITES. THIS PRACTICE, WHICH SEEMS VERY VIOLENT, ACTUALLY OCCURS WITHOUT PAIN; OFTEN THE VICTIM CONTINUES TO SLEEP AS IF NOTHING IS HAPPENING.

ACROBATIC fleas

FLEAS ARE EXCELLENT JUMPERS BECAUSE THEIR LAST PAIR OF LEGS IS HIGHLY DEVELOPED. THEY ARE ABLE TO PERFORM AS MANY AS 30,000 JUMPS IN A ROW WITHOUT STOPPING!

AGGRESSIVE Females

IT IS WELL KNOWN THAT MOSQUITOES SUCK BLOOD, BUT ONLY FEMALES HAVE MOUTHPARTS MADE FOR STINGING. THE BLOOD IS NECESSARY FOR THEM TO MATURE THEIR EGGS.

Tiny... INVADERS!

WHEN A PARASITE IS SMALLER THAN 0.04 IN (1 MM), WE DO NOT EVEN NOTICE ITS PRESENCE. HOWEVER, TINY MITES, RELATIVES OF SPIDERS AND TICKS, ARE JUST ABOUT EVERYWHERE, AND WE LIVE WITH THEM ON A DAILY BASIS.

Hunting for SPIDERS!

EVEN LARGE SPIDERS ARE NOT SAFE. THEY MUST GUARD AGAINST THE RED-WINGED WASP, WHICH TRIES TO IMPLANT ITS EGG IN THEIR ABDOMEN. TO DO SO, IT PARALYZES THE SPIDER, WHICH STAYS ALIVE LONG ENOUGH FOR THE LARVA TO EAT IT AND BECOME AN ADULT.

RISKY waters!

LEECHES LIVE IN PUDDLES AND SWAMPS, WAITING FOR A WARM-BLOODED HOST TO COME BY SO THEY CAN ATTACH THEMSELVES VIA A SUCKER AND THEN INCISE ITS SKIN BEFORE SUCKING ITS BLOOD.

CUCKOO

THE CUCKOO IS A PARASITE-OF NESTS. INSTEAD OF BUILDING HER OWN, THE FEMALE DEPOSITS HER EGG IN THE NEST OF ANOTHER SPECIES. AS SOON AS IT HATCHES, THE CHICK GETS RID OF THE OTHER EGGS IN THE NEST IN ORDER TO HAVE THE ATTENTION OF THE ADOPTIVE PARENTS ALL TO ITSELF!

LOVING PARENTS

Some strategies adopted by animals ensure the survival of their young.

There are many lessons passed on by parents, such as how to build a shelter, hunt prey, or protect oneself from predators, but some methods of caring for the young are very special!

Prescient SPIDERS

THE WOLF SPIDER PUTS ITS EGGS IN A KIND OF BACKPACK, STRAPS IT TO ITS BODY, AND CARRIES IT, THUS KEEPING THE EGGS OUT OF HARM'S WAY.

Mom ALLIGATOR

IT LAYS ITS EGGS IN A NEST BUILT FROM DECAYING PLANTS. THIS COMPOST PRODUCES HEAT, WHICH ENSURES THE OPTIMAL TEMPERATURE FOR THE EGGS BOTH DAY AND NIGHT.

The sacrifice of the mother OCTOPUS

AFTER LAYING UP TO 200,000 EGGS, THE FEMALE OCTOPUS PROTECTS THEM FOR TWO MONTHS WITHOUT LEAVING EVEN TO FEED. BECAUSE OF THIS SACRIFICE, HOWEVER, THE MOTHER OCTOPUS USUALLY DIES AFTER THE EGGS HATCH.

Protective PARENTS

TO PROTECT ITS YOUNG FROM SNAKES, THE SULAWESI HORNBILL BUILDS ITS NEST INSIDE A HOLLOW TREE AND THEN WALLS OFF THE ENTRANCE, LEAVING THE FEMALE AND CHICKS INSIDE FOR TWO MONTHS. FROM A SMALL HOLE, THE DAD PASSES FOOD TO THE LITTLE FAMILY.

Dad CLOWN FISH

IT IS THE MALE WHO TAKES RESPONSIBILITY FOR THE HATCHLINGS: HE PROTECTS THE NEST AND VENTILATES THE EGGS WITH HIS FINS TO ENSURE OXYGEN-RICH WATER AT ALL TIMES UNTIL THE HATCHLINGS ARE BORN, WHICH OCCURS AFTER ABOUT A WEEK.

Dad HIPPOCAMPUS

THE MALE SEAHORSE HAS A POUCH ON ITS ABDOMEN INSIDE WHICH THE FEMALE DEPOSITS EGGS. THE MALE WILL PROTECT AND FEED THE APPROXIMATELY 1,000 YOUNG UNTIL THEY ARE READY TO EMERGE.

Daddy EMU

EMU CHICKS HAVE A TRULY LOVING FATHER: NOT ONLY DOES HE FAST AND NEVER LEAVE THE NEST, BUT AFTER HATCHING, HE KEEPS THE CHICKS WITH HIM FOR SEVEN MONTHS, TEACHING THEM ALL THE TRICKS OF FINDING FOOD AND DEFENDING THEMSELVES FROM PREDATORS.

ASIAN ELEPHANT

ITS EARS AND TUSKS ARE SMALLER THAN THAT OF ITS AFRICAN RELATIVES. IT HAS A VERY LONG GESTATION OF 20-22 MONTHS, AT THE END OF WHICH ONLY ONE BABY IS BORN.

BIOLUMINESCENT ANIMALS

The ability of an organism to glow with its own light is called bioluminescence.

Although it may appear to be a superpower, underlying the phenomenon is actually a chemical reaction that takes place inside the bodies of very different animals. The light produced can range from blue to purple to greenish-yellow and, more rarely, to red.

A Great ADVANTAGE!

THE ABILITY TO TURN ON A LIGHT, EVEN A SMALL ONE, IN THE DARKNESS IS VERY USEFUL; ORGANISMS CAN MORE EASILY FIND FOOD OR A MATE, OR DAZZLE A PREDATOR AND HAVE TIME TO ESCAPE.

MONKFISH

THE DEEP-SEA ANGLERFISH HAS A LONG FILAMENT ON ITS FOREHEAD THAT ENDS IN AN LURE CONTAINING GLOWING BACTERIA. THIS DEVIOUS LURE IS USED TO ATTRACT CURIOUS PREY RIGHT IN FRONT OF ITS LARGE MOUTH.

An Unexpected SPECTACLE

...THAT IS PROVIDED BY MOST OCEAN ORGANISMS LIVING BETWEEN 656 AND 3,280 FT (200-1,000 M) DEEP: FISH, BACTERIA, SQUID, AND JELLYFISH BRING FLASHES OF LIGHT TO THE OTHERWISE DARK DEPTHS.

What a STRATEGY!

THE SOUTHERN LANTERN SHARK MANAGES TO MAKE ITSELF ALMOST INVISIBLE BY DISGUISING ITS SHADOW. IT ACHIEVES THIS BY LIGHTING UP BRIGHT DOTS ALONG THE SIDES OF ITS BODY.

A blinding WEAPON!

THE VAMPIRE SQUID, WHICH HAS NO INK SACS TO SPRAY AT ENEMIES, EXPELS A VERY STICKY BIOLUMINESCENT MUCUS. THIS SUDDEN LIGHT IN THE ABYSSAL DARKNESS CONFUSES PREDATORS.

Sparkling WATER

DURING WARM SUMMER NIGHTS, THE WATER IN SOME LAGOONS SPARKLES WITH AN ALMOST MAGICAL BLUE GLOW. PRODUCING IT ARE MILLIONS OF MICROSCOPIC ORGANISMS CALLED DINOFLAGELLATES THAT, WHEN DISTURBED, EMIT LIGHT THAT CREATES THIS NATURAL SPECTACLE.

What about on LAND?

AMONG THE FEW TERRESTRIAL BIOLUMINESCENT ORGANISMS, SURELY THE BEST KNOWN ARE FIREFLIES. THEY USE FLASHES OF LIGHT TO ATTRACT PARTNERS. HOWEVER, TO AVOID CONFUSION, EACH SPECIES HAS ITS OWN DISTINCT FLASHING PATTERN!

CUTTLEFISH

IT HAS 10 APPENDAGES: 8 ARMS OF EQUAL LENGTH AND 2 TENTACLES. SIZE RANGES FROM SMALL TO MEDIUM-LARGE; THE LARGEST DISCOVERED WAS 19.69 IN (50 CM) LONG AND WEIGHED 26.45 LB (12 KG).

SPIDERS AND SCORPIONS

Spiders and scorpions are among the most feared animals. Both are carnivores and hunt for small animals.

Most spiders weave webs to trap prey and then use their sharp fangs to inject venom. Scorpions, on the other hand, use two pincers to catch prey and then a painful stinger on the tip of the tail to kill it.

Don't call us BUGS!

SPIDERS AND SCORPIONS BELONG TO THE ARACHNID GROUP, EASILY DISTINGUISHED FROM INSECTS BECAUSE THEY HAVE EIGHT LEGS (INSTEAD OF SIX) AND LACK WINGS AND ANTENNAE.

A giant SCORPION

THE GIANT FOREST SCORPION IS BELIEVED TO BE THE LARGEST SPECIES CURRENTLY IN EXISTENCE, THANKS TO ITS LENGTH OF 9 IN (23 CM).

On an empty STOMACH!

SCORPIONS GENERALLY FEED EVERY TWO WEEKS, BUT THEY CAN ALSO SURVIVE FOR LONG PERIODS BETWEEN MEALS. SOME SPECIES CAN GO AS LONG AS 6 TO 12 MONTHS WITHOUT EATING!

What an amazing TECHNIQUE!

THE SCORPION GRABS ITS PREY WITH ITS PINCERS, THEN TIPS IT FORWARD AND STRIKES IT WITH THE VENOMOUS TIP OF ITS TAIL.

Harmless, and even HELPFUL

THE VAST MAJORITY OF SPIDERS ARE NOT ONLY HARMLESS TO HUMANS, THEY ALSO PERFORM AN IMPORTANT TASK: THEY LIMIT POPULATIONS OF INSECTS HARMFUL TO AGRICULTURE. A SPIDER CAN CATCH HUNDREDS OF SMALL FLIES IN A SINGLE DAY!

Silk HANDYMAN

ALTHOUGH NOT ALL SPIDERS BUILD WEBS, EACH SPECIES PRODUCES SILK, A FLEXIBLE FIBER THAT IS FIVE TIMES STRONGER THAN STEEL. WITH IT THEY CAN CLIMB, CATCH THEMSELVES IF THEY FALL, CREATE EGG SACS, WRAP UP PREY, AND MUCH MORE.

45,000

THE NUMBER OF SPIDER SPECIES CURRENTLY KNOWN, FOUND IN HABITATS AROUND THE WORLD.

JUMPING SPIDER

MOST SPIDERS HAVE EIGHT EYES, BUT THEY DO NOT HAVE VERY GOOD EYESIGHT. AN EXCEPTION IS THE JUMPING SPIDER, WHICH CAN SEE MORE COLORS THAN HUMANS AND CAN SPOT PREY 12-16 IN (30-40 CM) AWAY.

HOW ANIMALS COMMUNICATE

It is surprising how many ways animals can communicate, even without sound.

Animals are constantly sending signals, which we are still learning to decipher. Many species have bizarre ways to signal all kinds of messages, with noises or their bodies.

Say it... WITH A KISS

ANIMALS LIVING IN GROUPS DEVELOP A VERY COMPLEX LANGUAGE. PRAIRIE DOGS GREET EACH OTHER WITH A KISS, AND TO WARN OF DANGER, THEY USE 25 DIFFERENT SOUNDS, ONE FOR EACH TYPE OF PREDATOR IN THE VICINITY.

Say it... WITH LEGS

MANY INSECTS DO NOT USE THEIR VOICES TO COMMUNICATE. THE MALE GRASSHOPPER RUBS ITS LEGS, WINGS, OR OTHER BODY PARTS TOGETHER TO PRODUCE A HIGH-PITCHED SQUEAL TO CALL TO FEMALES.

Say it... WITH THE TAIL

TO WARN FAMILY MEMBERS THAT THERE IS DANGER, THE BEAVER RESORTS TO TAPPING ITS FLASHY, FLAT, SCALE-COVERED TAIL REPEATEDLY ON THE SURFACE OF THE WATER.

Say it... WITH WAVES

ELEPHANTS EXCHANGE MESSAGES USING INFRASOUND, WHICH ARE VERY LOW SOUND WAVES NOT AUDIBLE TO OUR EARS. IT IS ESTIMATED THAT AN AFRICAN ELEPHANT CAN HEAR A MATE 31 MILES (50 KM) AWAY.

Say it... WITH SONG

IT IS KNOWN THAT OLDER MALE GORILLAS, CALLED SILVERBACKS, STAND AND BEAT THEIR CHESTS TO SHOW THEIR POWER. HOWEVER, IT HAS ALSO BEEN FOUND THAT IF THEY SING WHILE CHEWING IT MEANS THAT THEY DO NOT WANT TO BE DISTURBED DURING A MEAL.

Say it... TO A FRIEND

WHEN DAY GECKOS WANT A SNACK, THEY NOD THEIR HEADS TO CICADAS, INSECTS THAT DIGEST SAP AND EXCRETE IT AS A SUGARY LIQUID DIRECTLY AT THE GECKOS' MOUTHS.

Say it... WITH POOP

WHITE RHINOS HAVE POOR EYESIGHT, SO THEY RELY ON THEIR SENSE OF SMELL. THEY USE FECES PILES AS A KIND OF BULLETIN BOARD WHERE THEY LEAVE MESSAGES TO LET EVERYONE KNOW IF THEY ARE SICK, IF THEY ARE LOOKING FOR A MATE, AND SO ON.

WOLF

COMMUNICATION BETWEEN WOLVES CAN TAKE PLACE THROUGH SOUND. IN FACT, HOWLING IS USED DURING A HUNT TO STAY IN CONTACT WITH THE REST OF THE PACK, EVEN AT GREAT DISTANCES.

MIGRATORY ANIMALS

Migrations are journeys, sometimes epic, made by animals moving together from one place to another.

Animals can go so far as to cross entire continents to reach places where they can find ideal conditions for abundant food or to give birth to offspring.

An internal COMPASS

BIRDS AND SEA TURTLES ARE ABLE TO ORIENT THEMSELVES BY EARTH'S MAGNETIC FIELD, JUST AS IF THEY HAD A COMPASS, USING SIGNALS THAT GUIDE THEIR MIGRATIONS.

From Earth TO THE MOON

IN ITS LIFETIME, THE ARCTIC TERN TRAVELS SIX TIMES THE DISTANCE BETWEEN EARTH AND THE MOON, EACH YEAR FLYING BETWEEN THE ARCTIC CIRCLE, WHERE IT BREEDS, AND ANTARCTICA, WHERE IT SPENDS WINTERS.

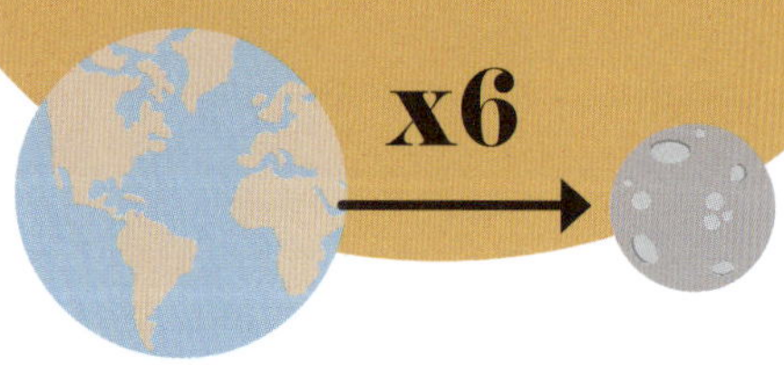

All in FORMATION

MANY FLOCKS OF BIRDS, SUCH AS GEESE, FLY IN A V FORMATION DURING MIGRATION. THIS ARRANGEMENT REDUCES AIR RESISTANCE AND SAVES ENERGY. THE LEAD BIRD, HOWEVER, BECOMES FATIGUED AND MUST PERIODICALLY BE REPLACED BY ANOTHER.

10 MILLION

THE NUMBER OF YELLOW FRUIT BATS THAT, EACH YEAR AT THE BEGINNING OF THE RAINY SEASON, TRAVEL FROM CONGO TO ZAMBIA, MAKING A 1,243 MILE (2,000-KM) JOURNEY. WHEN THEY SOAR, THE HUGE FLOCKS DARKEN THE SKY.

On the road for the LITTLE ONES

AMONG MAMMALS, THE ONES WITH THE LONGEST DISPLACEMENT ARE HUMPBACK WHALES. THEY SWIM ANNUALLY FROM ANTARCTICA TO THE WARM SEAS OF THE TROPICS TO BREED.

All AGREED!

WHEN THEY MIGRATE, LOCUSTS FORM A HUGE SWARM. COMPRISED OF BILLIONS OF INSECTS, THEY ACT AS ONE, MAKING, FOR EXAMPLE, QUICK DECISIONS ABOUT WHICH DIRECTION TO TAKE.

WILDEBEEST

THE GREAT MASS WILDEBEEST MIGRATION INVOLVES MILLIONS OF WILDEBEEST CROSSING TANZANIA AND KENYA EACH YEAR IN SEARCH OF GREEN PASTURES AND WATER.

ALL THE BEARS IN THE WORLD

Bears are large mammals widespread through much of the world.

They are found throughout North America, South America, Europe, and Asia, from the frozen lands of the Arctic to warm tropical forests.

8 different SPECIES

LET'S COUNT THEM TOGETHER! THERE ARE ASIATIC BLACK BEARS, BROWN BEARS, GIANT PANDAS, NORTH AMERICAN BLACK BEARS, POLAR BEARS, SLOTH BEARS, SPECTACLED BEARS, AND THE SMALLEST, SUN BEARS.

Bamboo LOVERS!

PANDAS SPEND MORE THAN 12 HOURS EACH DAY BINGING ON BAMBOO. THEY EAT 22-44 LB (10-20 KG) OF IT, USING A SPECIAL FRONT PAW "FINGER" THAT IS ACTUALLY A MODIFIED WRIST BONE.

Like a VACUUM

WITH ITS SPECIAL LOWER LIP, THE SLOTH BEAR CREATES A KIND OF TUBE TO SUCK UP LARGE AMOUNTS OF TERMITES AND OTHER INSECTS THAT MAKE UP 90 PERCENT OF ITS DIET.

To each its own DIET!

ALL BEARS ARE CONSIDERED OMNIVORES, ALTHOUGH EACH SPECIES HAS A FAVORITE DIET: THE POLAR BEAR, FOR EXAMPLE, EATS MAINLY SEALS, AND SLOTH BEARS REALLY LIKE TERMITES.

Winter is COMING...

IN REGIONS OF THE NORTHERN HEMISPHERE, FOOD IS SCARCE IN THE WINTER, SO BEARS ENTER A STATE OF TORPOR DURING WHICH THEY DO NOT EAT, DRINK, OR "DO THEIR BUSINESS." THEY CAN STAY LIKE THIS UP TO 100 DAYS, THANKS TO FAT RESERVES ACCUMULATED DURING THE SUMMER.

How good this SEAL SMELLS!

AN EXCELLENT SENSE OF SMELL IS A CHARACTERISTIC OF ALL BEARS, BUT POLAR BEARS ARE REALLY SPECIAL: THEY CAN SMELL THE BREATHING HOLES OF SEALS IN THE ICE FROM ALMOST .62 MILE (1 KM) AWAY.

Not quite WHITE

THE THICK FUR OF THE POLAR BEAR IS ACTUALLY TRANSLUCENT; IT APPEARS WHITE TO US BECAUSE IT REFLECTS VISIBLE LIGHT. ITS SKIN, ON THE OTHER HAND, IS BLACK BECAUSE THAT WAY IT CAN ABSORB THE SUN'S WEAK HEAT RAYS.

Not only BLACK

NORTH AMERICAN BLACK BEARS IN ACTUALITY HAVE A WIDER RANGE OF COLORS: BLACK, BROWN, CINNAMON, BLOND, GRAY, AND EVEN WHITE.

BROWN BEAR

IT WEIGHS 220 TO 1,543 LB (100 TO 700 KG), AND ITS LARGEST MEMBERS CONTEND WITH THE POLAR BEAR FOR THE TITLE OF THE WORLD'S LARGEST LAND CARNIVORE.

AQUATIC MAMMALS

They are warm-blooded animals that give birth to pups and nurse them.

There are 130 species of marine mammals living in Earth's seas and oceans today–for example, seals, sea lions, whales, dolphins, porpoises, manatees, sea otters, and even polar bears.

BREATHING!

UNLIKE FISH, THESE MAMMALS CANNOT GET OXYGEN FROM WATER BUT MUST RISE TO THE SURFACE TO BREATHE AIR.

What BIG TEETH!

YOU CAN RECOGNIZE A WALRUS BY THE 3-FT (1-M) LONG TUSKS THAT BOTH MALES AND FEMALES HAVE. THEY ARE USED TO MOVE ON ICE AND TO DEFEND THEMSELVES FROM PREDATORS.

Not paws BUT FINS

FOR THIS CHARACTERISTIC, SEALS, SEA LIONS, AND WALRUSES BELONG TO THE PINNIPED GROUP.

The LARGEST

IS THE BLUE WHALE, WHICH CAN REACH 98.4 FT (30 M) IN LENGTH AND WEIGHS AS MUCH AS 23 ELEPHANTS, 230 COWS, OR 1,800 HUMANS.

The unicorns OF THE SEA

THEY ARE THE NARWHALS, AMONG THE RAREST AND STRANGEST OF AQUATIC MAMMALS. MALES HAVE EARNED THE NICKNAME BECAUSE OF THE LONG SPIRAL TOOTH THAT PIERCES THE UPPER LIP DURING GROWTH AND CAN BE UP TO 10 FT (3 M) LONG.

Do you know how to distinguish between SEA LIONS AND SEALS?

SEA LIONS HAVE SMALL EARS ON THEIR HEADS AND CAN ROTATE THEIR HIND FLIPPERS FORWARD TO WALK ON LAND. SEALS HAVE ONLY TWO SMALL HOLES AS EARS, AND THEIR HIND FLIPPERS CANNOT ROTATE, SO THEY MOVE ON LAND WITH DIFFICULTY.

CALIFORNIA SEA LION

A SEA LION THAT LIVES ALONG THE COAST OF THE NORTH PACIFIC.

It's all in THE TAIL

DOLPHINS CAN SWIM AT GREAT SPEED AND MAKE LONG LEAPS OUT OF THE WATER BECAUSE THEY USE THEIR STRONG TAIL AS A THRUSTER.

POLYPS AND JELLYFISH

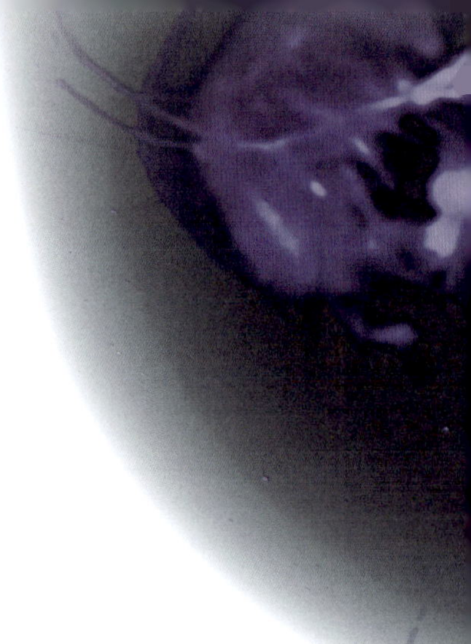

Polyps and jellyfish are aquatic animals with tentacles capable of releasing a toxic, stinging substance upon touch.

They belong to the cnidarian family and are also called coelenterates because their body is, essentially, an empty sack.

At the mercy OF THE WAVES

JELLYFISH MOVE BY RHYTHMICALLY PULSING THEIR BODIES, BUT WITH NO REAL CONTROL OVER WHERE THEY ARE HEADING. MOST OF THE TIME, THEY ARE CARRIED ALONG BY THE CURRENT OF THE WATER.

Tentacles WIDE OPEN

IN POLYPS THE TENTACLES SURROUND THE MOUTH BUT TEND UPWARD, SO THE BODY RESEMBLES THE SHAPE OF A VESSEL. VERY OFTEN THESE ANIMALS LIVE ATTACHED TO THE SEABED WITHOUT MOVING.

Inside CORALS...

...LIVE COLONIES OF POLYPS THAT BUILD A CALCIUM CARBONATE SKELETON AS PROTECTION. THEIR SLOW AND STEADY WORK HAS OVER TIME PRODUCED CORAL REEFS, INCLUDING AUSTRALIA'S, WHICH IS 1,429 MILES (2,300 KM) LONG.

Older than DINOSAURS!

COELENTERATES ARE VERY ANCIENT ANIMALS. THEY HAVE EXISTED FOR MORE THAN 500 MILLION YEARS, WHICH IS LONG BEFORE DINOSAURS APPEARED ON EARTH.

NETTLE JELLYFISH

A CARNIVOROUS JELLYFISH THAT LIVES IN THE COLDEST OCEANS.

A gelatinous BODY

THE JELLYFISH'S BODY IS GELATINOUS AS IT IS MADE OF 97 PERCENT WATER. IT IS USUALLY SHAPED LIKE AN UMBRELLA, AND FROM THE UNDERSIDE HANG NUMEROUS LONG TENTACLES SURROUNDING THE MOUTH.

Stinging power IN ACTION!

THE STINGING POWER IS DUE TO THOUSANDS OF SPECIAL CELLS ON THE TENTACLES THAT, EVEN IF BARELY TOUCHED, SHOOT OUT SHARP FILAMENTS FULL OF TOXINS THAT ARE CAPABLE OF PIERCING THE SKIN.

ANIMALS WITH WINGS

Flight is possible because of special structures called wings.

There are different types of wings in the animal world; some are very strong, others lighter than a sheet of paper. They are found in only three kinds of animals: birds, insects, and bats, which are the only mammals capable of flight.

Hands TO FLY

IN ALL OF THE MORE THAN 1,400 SPECIES OF BATS, THE WINGS ARE FORMED BY THE FOREARM AND HAND BONES, WHICH ARE THIN AND ELONGATED LIKE THE SLATS OF AN UMBRELLA.

Down TO EARTH

ALL BIRDS HAVE WINGS, BUT NOT ALL OF THEM CAN FLY. THE OSTRICH, EMU, NANDU, CASSOWARY, AND KIWI MOVE BY RUNNING ON STURDY HIND LEGS. PENGUINS ALSO CANNOT FLY AND USE THEIR WINGS TO SWIM.

With feet IN THE AIR

BATS HAVE ADAPTED SO WELL TO FLIGHT THAT THEIR BODIES DO NOT SUPPORT THEM WHEN THEY ARE ON THE GROUND. THEY HAVE TO HANG UPSIDE DOWN WHEN NOT FLYING, AND TO TAKE FLIGHT THEY JUST HAVE TO LET THEMSELVES FALL.

A very fast FLIGHT

A DRAGONFLY'S FOUR WINGS CAN MOVE INDEPENDENTLY AND FLAP UP TO 30 TIMES PER SECOND. SUCH RAPID MOVEMENT ENABLES THEM TO TAKE OFF, FLY BACKWARD, AND CHANGE DIRECTION WITH INCREDIBLE AGILITY.

Prehistoric ANCESTORS

IN BIRDS, WINGS ARE THE RESULT OF A MODIFICATION OF THE FORELIMBS OF THEIR DINOSAUR ANCESTORS.

HUMMINGBIRD

IT IS THE ONLY BIRD THAT CAN FLY IN ANY DIRECTION, EVEN BACKWARD.

Very Small WINGS

INSECTS USUALLY HAVE FOUR WINGS, BUT IN FLIES AND MOSQUITOES, ONE PAIR IS EXTREMELY SMALL; THEY ARE CALLED HALTERES. THEY ARE USED TO CONTROL LANDING AND TAKEOFF AND TO MAINTAIN BALANCE DURING FLIGHT.

Very big WINGS

THE WINGS OF THE ALBATROSS, AT A LENGTH OF UP TO 11.5 FT (3.5 M), TOGETHER WITH THEIR LONG, NARROW SHAPE, ALLOW THE BIRD TO TRAVEL LONG DISTANCES WITHOUT TIRING.

SOCIAL ANIMALS

Many animals live in large colonies in which individuals cooperate to perform various tasks.

Social animals help raise the young, defend the group, and provide food for all. For these animals, it is cooperation that makes them strong!

The pack IS POWERFUL!

LIONS ARE THE ONLY FELINES THAT LIVE IN PACKS, CONSISTING MAINLY OF FEMALES, IN WHICH EACH MEMBER PARTICIPATES IN HUNTING, DEFENDING TERRITORY, AND CARING FOR CUBS.

To each its own TASK

MEERKATS LIVE IN GROUPS OF 20 TO 30 INDIVIDUALS INSIDE BURROWS DUG IN THE GROUND. A FEW DOMINANT INDIVIDUALS LEAD THE GROUP, WHILE THE OTHERS TAKE ON VARIOUS TASKS SUCH AS BEING SENTINELS, BABYSITTERS, AND HUNTERS.

The queen's GUARDS

IF A PREDATOR TRIES TO ENTER THE BURROW OF A NAKED MOLE RAT COLONY, "SOLDIERS" WILL GATHER TO BLOCK THE ENTRANCE. THEY WILL FIGHT BRAVELY TO SAVE THEIR QUEEN, WHO IS THE ONLY FEMALE THAT CAN REPRODUCE.

At your majesty's ORDERS!

IN SOCIAL INSECTS, ONLY ONE FEMALE REPRODUCES, AND SHE IS CALLED THE QUEEN.THIS HAPPENS, FOR EXAMPLE, AMONG ANTS, BEES, AND TINY TERMITES, WHOSE QUEEN HAS A SWOLLEN ABDOMEN ABOUT 4 IN (10 CM) LONG THAT MAKES IT IMPOSSIBLE FOR HER TO MOVE.

How TALKATIVE!

AMONG SOCIAL ANIMALS, COMMUNICATION IS VERY IMPORTANT. RESEARCHERS HAVE FOUND THAT ELEPHANTS USE MORE THAN 70 TYPES OF VOCAL SOUNDS AND 160 VISUAL AND TACTILE SIGNALS, INCLUDING EXPRESSIONS AND GESTURES.

DOLPHIN

IN THE SEAS, THE DOLPHIN LIVES IN SCHOOLS AND COOPERATES IN FISHING. FIVE TO SIX DOLPHINS WORK TOGETHER TO GATHER FISH BY HERDING THEM. THEN, THEY LINE UP TO CREATE A WAVE THAT PUSHES THE FISH TOWARD THE SHORE, WHERE THEY BECOME AN EASY MEAL FOR THE GROUP.

The societies of PRIMATES

PRIMATES, INCLUDING HUMANS, KNOW HOW TO CREATE COMPLEX SOCIETIES. GORILLAS, FOR EXAMPLE, WORK TOGETHER IN FAMILY GROUPS FOR THE COMMON CARE OF THEIR YOUNG AND THE PROTECTION OF ALL.

A very organized SOCIETY

EACH MEMBER OF A WOLF PACK PLAYS A SPECIFIC ROLE, FROM HUNTING TO CARING FOR THE PUPS, FOLLOWING THE ORDERS OF THE ALPHA MALE AND FEMALE, WHO ARE IN CHARGE OF THE GROUP.

Everyone get to WORK!

SOME "SOCIAL" SPIDERS WORK TOGETHER TO BUILD HUGE WEBS, SOMETIMES MILES WIDE, THAT CATCH FAR MORE PREY THAN A SINGLE WEB COULD.

OCEAN FISH

The ocean is really full of fish!

Some live alone, while others gather in groups called schools that can consist of thousands of individuals. Fish are found at various depths and in waters of different temperatures. The oceans are so large that each species can find its ideal living conditions.

500 MILLION years ago

FOSSILS TELL US THAT FISH APPEARED MORE THAN 500 MILLION YEARS AGO DURING THE CAMBRIAN PERIOD. THE OLDEST WERE JAWLESS, SO THEY COULD NOT BITE AND COULD ONLY SUCK IN THEIR PREY.

Surviving OUT OF WATER?

PERIOPHTHALMUS, ALSO CALLED MUDSKIPPERS, ARE ABLE TO KEEP THEIR GILLS, THE ORGANS THAT ALLOW FISH TO BREATHE UNDERWATER, MOIST FOR A LONG TIME. THEY CAN SURVIVE MORE THAN A DAY IN THE MUD.

Does a fish DRINK?

UNLIKE FRESHWATER FISH, SALTWATER FISH DRINK WATER TO COMPENSATE FOR THE WATER EXPELLED FROM THEIR BODIES THROUGH THE GILLS AND SKIN DUE TO THE SALINITY OF THE SEA.

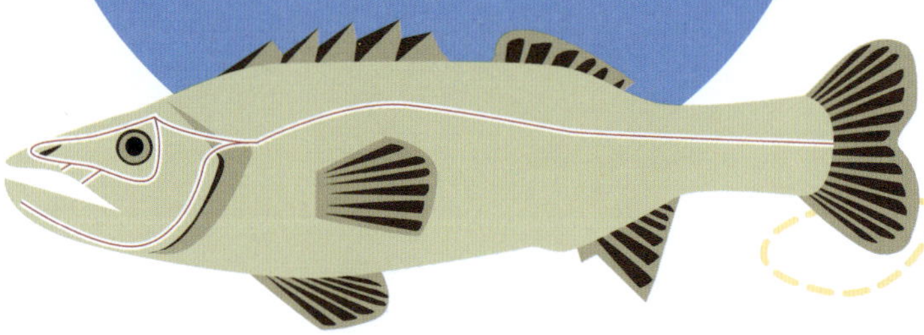

How to live BELOW ZERO

ICEFISH CAN WITHSTAND THE SUBZERO TEMPERATURES OF THE ANTARCTIC SEA THANKS TO A SPECIAL ANTIFREEZE SUBSTANCE IN THEIR BLOOD.

The sixth sense OF FISH

THE LATERAL LINE, WHICH RUNS ALONG THE BODY ON BOTH SIDES, ALLOWS FISH TO SENSE ANY SMALL SHIFT IN THE WATER AROUND THEM.

YELLOWFIN TUNA

ALL FISH ARE COLD-BLOODED ANIMALS–THAT IS, THEIR TEMPERATURE IS EQUAL TO THAT OF THE WATER. TUNA, HOWEVER, CAN HAVE A BODY TEMPERATURE AROUND 86°F (30°C) DESPITE SWIMMING IN COLD WATER BELOW 50°F (10°C).

It was extinct... OR WAS IT?

THE COELACANTH IS A LARGE FISH DISCOVERED ONLY IN THE LAST CENTURY. IT IS CONSIDERED A "LIVING FOSSIL" BECAUSE IT BELONGS TO A GROUP THAT WAS THOUGHT TO HAVE GONE EXTINCT WITH THE DINOSAURS, MORE THAN 66 MILLION YEARS AGO.

A long-lived FISH

IT IS NOT EASY TO CALCULATE HOW LONG FISH LIVE, BUT SCIENTISTS HAVE DISCOVERED THAT THE ORANGE ROUGHY CAN LIVE UP TO 150 YEARS, AND IT IS CERTAINLY ONE OF THE LONGEST-LIVING FISH IN EXISTENCE TODAY.

FRESHWATER FISH

Even the fresh waters of the planet are inhabited by fish.

Unlike those of fish in the ocean, the environments of freshwater fish are less varied, but the species are still diverse. Some live in the tumultuous waters of streams, others in calmer areas, such as the waters of large rivers and lakes. And some even live in swamps and marshes.

About 10,000...

...FRESHWATER SPECIES LIVE WORLDWIDE, SWIMMING IN ENVIRONMENTS THAT MAKE UP LESS THAN 3 PERCENT OF EARTH'S AVAILABLE WATER SUPPLY.

A Refined PALATE

CATFISH HAVE A MORE REFINED TASTE THAN OURS. THIS IS DUE TO THE 27,000 TASTE BUDS SCATTERED ALL OVER THE BODY, WHILE WE HAVE ABOUT 7,000, ONLY ON THE TONGUE.

They never DRINK!

FRESHWATER FISH ARE NEVER THIRSTY BECAUSE WATER NATURALLY PASSES THROUGH THEIR BODIES, THUS ELIMINATING THE NEED TO DRINK.

So PARTICULAR

TROUT LIVE ONLY IN STREAMS AND LAKES WITH CLEAR, COOL, AND VERY CLEAN WATER.

Without SCALES!

NOT ALL FISH ARE COVERED WITH SCALES. THE STURGEON, FOR EXAMPLE, HAS FIVE ROWS OF BONY SHIELDS RUNNING THE LENGTH OF ITS BODY.

PIRANHA

JUST SAYING ITS NAME MAKES US AFRAID, BUT THE RED-BELLIED PIRANHA IS ACTUALLY MORE A TIMID SCAVENGER THAN A RAVENOUS KILLER. IT IS UNLIKELY TO ATTACK HUMANS, PREFERRING INSECTS, WORMS, CRUSTACEANS, AND OTHER FISH.

A most useful ORGAN

THE SWIM BLADDER IS USEFUL FOR FISH TO REGULATE AT WHAT DEPTH THEY SWIM. THE AFRICAN BUTTERFLYFISH, SO NAMED BECAUSE ITS FINS ARE SO WIDE THAT THEY CAN MAKE SMALL FLIGHTS OUT OF THE WATER, USES ITS SWIM BLADDER AS A LUNG.

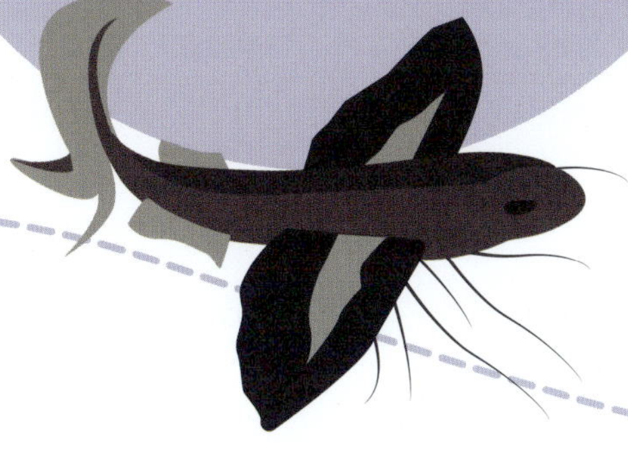

The SMALLEST...

THE FEMALE DWARF GOBY, *PAEDOCYPRIS PROGENETICA*, DISCOVERED ONLY IN 2006 IN THE DARK WATERS OF SOME SUMATRAN SWAMPS, BARELY REACHES .31 IN (8 MM) IN LENGTH.

BIZARRE FISH

An incredible amount of creatures live in the vast oceans.

Some are so strange and unusual that we can barely believe they really exist and wonder if they are instead a figment of our imagination. In fact, their strange shapes are solutions that some species have found in the course of their evolution.

A regal FISH

THE KING OF HERRINGS, OR GIANT OARFISH, IS A FISH REMINISCENT OF MYTHOLOGICAL SEA SERPENTS. IT IS A GOOD 33 FT (10 M) LONG AND HAS A PLUMED CROWN ON ITS HEAD, BUT ALSO A RED-COLORED DORSAL FIN THAT RUNS ALONG ITS BODY, LIKE A REGAL CLOAK.

A made-up FISH?

THE SUNFISH LOOKS LIKE AN INVENTED ANIMAL: IT IS ROUND AND FLAT, AND IT HAS A TINY MOUTH AND BIG EYES ON AN IMMENSE BODY, WHICH LOOKS EVEN BIGGER BECAUSE OF ITS TRUNCATED TAIL.

Beautiful but DANGEROUS!

THE BEAUTIFUL LIONFISH ATTRACTS ATTENTION, NOT SO MUCH FOR ITS FLASHY STRIPES AS FOR ITS ELEGANT PECTORAL FINS THAT FLOAT IN THE WATER. IT IS GOOD TO STEER CLEAR BECAUSE IT POSSESSES A POWERFUL VENOM, WHICH IT INJECTS WITH ITS 18 NEEDLE-LIKE DORSAL FINS.

An artistic FISH

ALL TRIGGERFISH LOOK LIKE LIVING PAINTINGS, BUT THE PICASSO TRIGGERFISH SURPASSES THEM ALL. NOT SURPRISINGLY, IT IS NAMED AFTER THE FAMOUS PAINTER BECAUSE, WITH ITS STRIKING COLORS AND INTRICATE PATTERNS, IT IS A TRUE MASTERPIECE OF NATURE.

Using the saw ON PREY!

THE SAWFISH USES ITS LONG SNOUT, OR ROSTRUM, WITH 2-INCH (5-CM) SCALES ON THE SIDES, TO CUT PREY IN HALF!

Like A STONE

WHEN AMONG THE ROCKS OF THE SEABED, THE STONE FISH BECOMES VIRTUALLY IMPOSSIBLE TO SEE. ITS BODY IS LUMPY, AND IT HAS THE ABILITY TO STAY STILL FOR HOURS ON END, LOOKING JUST LIKE A ROCK. ITS UGLINESS IS EQUAL TO ITS DANGER BECAUSE IT IS VERY POISONOUS.

PARROTFISH

AMONG THE MOST AMAZING FISH IN THE OCEAN IS THE PARROTFISH, OF WHICH 80 DIFFERENT SPECIES ARE KNOWN. IT GETS ITS NAME NOT SO MUCH BECAUSE OF ITS BRIGHT COLORS, BUT BECAUSE OF ITS MOUTH: ITS FUSED TEETH RESEMBLE THE BEAK OF A PARROT.

ANIMALS AT RISK OF EXTINCTION

Earth is home to a seemingly infinite variety of living things. This varies over time, with species disappearing and appearing.

Although extinction is a natural process, today the speed at which species are disappearing is 1,000 to 10,000 times faster than in the past, and the main cause is human beings.

Nearly 900 SPECIES...

HAVE GONE EXTINCT IN THE PAST 500 YEARS DUE TO HUMAN ACTIVITY, AND ONE IN FOUR MAMMALS AND ONE IN EIGHT BIRDS ARE AT HIGH RISK OF DISAPPEARING IN THE NEAR FUTURE.

The tiny HIPPOPOTAMUS

PERHAPS NOT EVERYONE KNOWS THAT THERE IS A PYGMY HIPPO, LESS THAN 3.28 FT (1 M) TALL AT THE SHOULDERS. ITS EXISTENCE IS THREATENED BY THE DESTRUCTION OF ITS FOREST HABITAT AND BY UNCONTROLLED HUNTING FOR ITS MEAT AND IVORY FROM ITS TUSKS.

Good NEWS!

THE MAURITIUS PINK PIGEON WAS ONE STEP AWAY FROM EXTINCTION. IN 1975 THERE WERE ONLY A DOZEN OR SO LEFT, BUT THANKS TO THE HARD WORK OF NATURALIST GERALD DURRELL, TODAY, AFTER HALF A CENTURY, THERE ARE ABOUT 400 INDIVIDUALS IN THE WILD.

A symbol of SALVATION!

THE FEW SURVIVING AREAS OF FOREST THAT COVER THE MAJOR ISLANDS OF THE PHILIPPINES ARE HOME TO THE LAST PHILIPPINE EAGLES. THIS RAPTOR HAS BEEN STRICTLY PROTECTED SINCE 1995 AND HAS BECOME THE COUNTRY'S NATIONAL BIRD.

What a DIFFICULT LIFE!

INTENSIVE FISHING AND LOSS OF BEACH HABITAT ARE MAKING LIFE DIFFICULT FOR THE MEDITERRANEAN MONK SEAL, ONCE WIDESPREAD IN THE MEDITERRANEAN.

A species COMEBACK

TOWARD THE END OF THE LAST CENTURY, NO MORE THAN A DOZEN MAURITIUS ECHO PARAKEETS SURVIVED, EXTERMINATED BY PREDATORS AND DISEASE. THE STRICT PROTECTION PROGRAM PUT IN PLACE HAS SAVED THE SPECIES, NOW REPRESENTED BY ABOUT 800 SPECIMENS.

IBERIAN LYNX

THE IBERIAN LYNX IS THE RAREST FELINE IN EUROPE. THE DECREASE IN ITS NATURAL PREY AND THE CONSTRUCTION OF HIGHWAYS AND RAILWAYS HAVE LED TO THIS ANIMAL BEING SERIOUSLY THREATENED.

SYMBIOSIS

To survive, sometimes it is best to rely on each other!

Some organisms create lasting "friendships" to gain advantages, and these relationships are called mutualistic symbioses. Sometimes the bond is so tight that survival would be jeopardized if either organism were to fail.

Gourmand ANTS

APHIDS ARE SMALL SAP-SUCKING INSECTS. THEY PRODUCE A SUGARY LIQUID THAT MANY SPECIES OF ANTS ARE FOND OF. TO OBTAIN IT, THE ANTS ENGAGE IN BREEDING AND PROTECTING THE APHIDS.

Tiny ALLIES

HUMANS ALSO HAVE A FUNDAMENTAL CONNECTION-WITH MICROORGANISMS THAT WE HOST IN OUR INTESTINES. THEY FORM BACTERIAL FLORA AND HELP US IN DIGESTION, METABOLISM, AND IMMUNE SYSTEM REGULATION, PROVIDING US WITH WELL-BEING.

The friendship of ALGAE and POLYPS

ZOOXANTHELLAE ARE MICROSCOPIC ALGAE THAT LIVE INSIDE THE POLYPS OF CORALS. THEY PROVIDE FOOD FOR THE CORAL, WHICH IN TURN, GIVE THEM A SHELTER IN WHICH TO LIVE.

An odd ALLIANCE

THERE EXISTS AN INTERESTING ALLIANCE BETWEEN SOUTH AMERICAN TARANTULAS AND TINY FROGS: THE TWO ANIMALS SHARE A BURROW. IN EXCHANGE FOR THE SPIDER'S PROTECTION, THE BRAVE AMPHIBIAN DEVOURS ANTS THAT THREATEN THE SPIDER'S EGGS.

Little fish and TENTACLES

CLOWNFISH LIVE AMONG THE STINGING TENTACLES OF SEA ANEMONES. THEY ARE IMMUNE TO THE ANEMONES' TOXINS, WHICH INSTEAD WARD OFF PREDATORS. IN RETURN, THE FISH RID THE ANEMONES OF PARASITES AND PROVIDE NUTRIENTS... WITH THEIR FECES.

The crocodile's DENTIST

THIS DANGEROUS ROLE IS PLAYED BY THE PLOVER, THE ONLY ANIMAL THAT CAN ENTER THE CROCODILE'S LARGE OPEN MOUTH WITHOUT DANGER. THE BIRD CLEANS THE CROCODILE'S TEETH, EATING THE SCRAPS OF MEAT STUCK BETWEEN THEM.

RED-BILLED OXPECKERS

THE RED-BILLED OXPECKER IS A SMALL AFRICAN BIRD THAT PERCHES ON LARGE SAVANNA HERBIVORES. IT DEVOURS THE HERBIVORES' PARASITES, RIDDING THEM OF MORE THAN 10,000 INSECT LARVAE OR 100 TICKS IN A SINGLE DAY!

PLANTS AND MUSHROOMS

-Chapter 2-

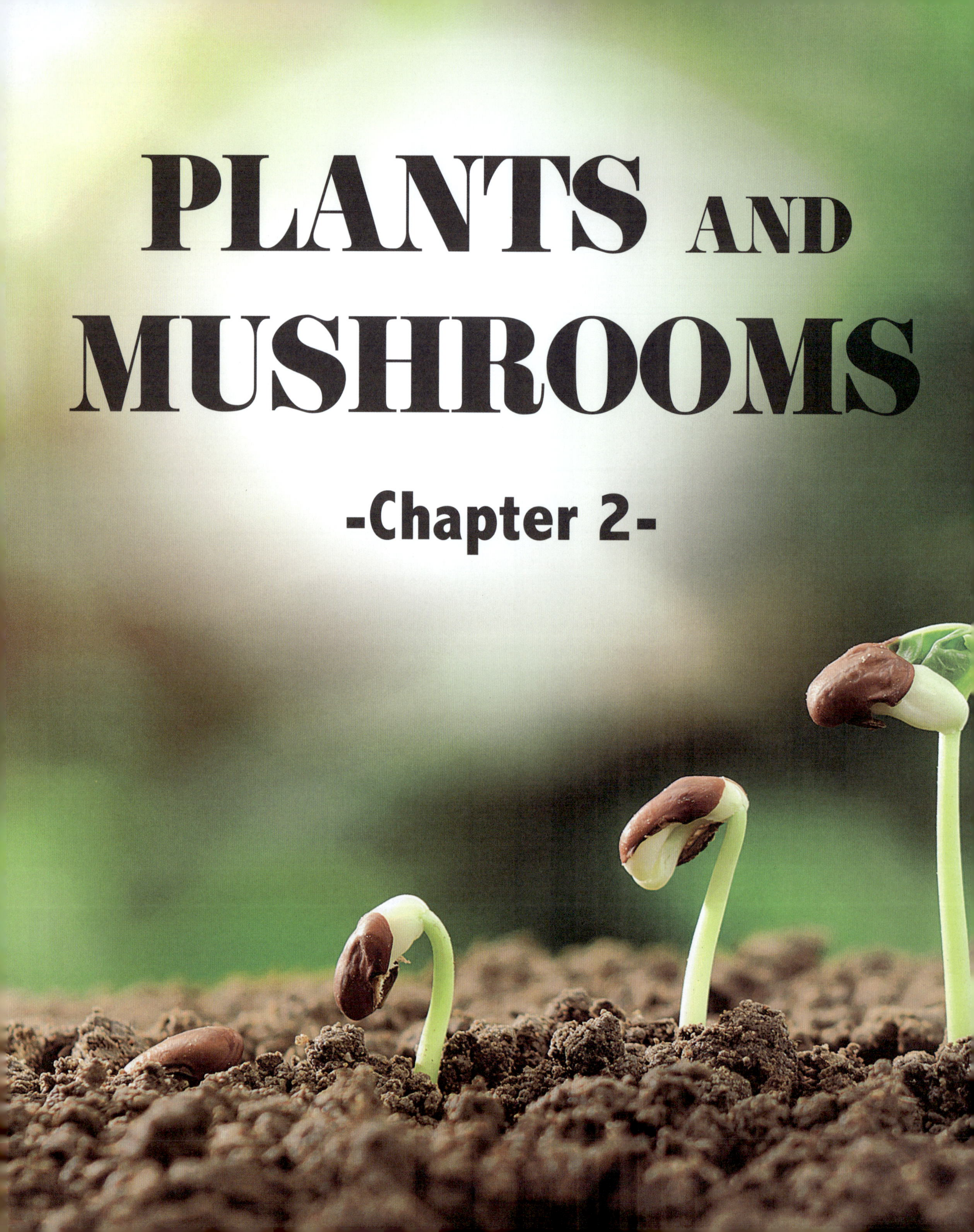

AQUATIC PLANTS

72,500

THE KNOWN SPECIES OF ALGAE.

They grow in water and are found in oceans, seas, lakes, rivers, and ponds.

Aquatic plants have developed special characteristics: floating leaves and roots can absorb oxygen and they have the ability to survive with little light. They play an important role in the ecosystem because they provide food and shelter for many animals and help keep the water clean by absorbing various pollutants.

CO_2

500 MILLION tons

OF CARBON DIOXIDE: BROWN ALGAE ARE ABLE TO ABSORB THIS INCREDIBLE AMOUNT OF GAS FROM THE ATMOSPHERE EACH YEAR. IT IS BELIEVED THAT THEY PLAY AN IMPORTANT ROLE IN CLIMATE CONTROL!

O_2

70 PERCENT

THE PERCENTAGE OF OXYGEN THAT COMES FROM AQUATIC PLANTS.

ALGAE

THE OLDEST AND MOST COMMON TYPE OF AQUATIC PLANT; EASY TO RECOGNIZE BY ITS SLIMY APPEARANCE AND THE ABSENCE OF ROOTS, STEMS, OR LEAVES.

RED ALGAE

IT LIVES MAINLY IN WARM SEAWATERS, AND THERE ARE ABOUT 4,000 SPECIES.

LEAVES of 16.5 ft

MANY AQUATIC PLANTS ARE BUOYANT AND POSSESS AIR-FILLED CAVITIES IN THEIR LEAVES AND STEMS. OTHERS, SUCH AS WATER LILIES, FLOAT BECAUSE OF THEIR ROUND, FLAT LEAVES UP TO 10 FT (3 M) WIDE.

LOTUS FLOWER

THE LOTUS FLOWER PRODUCES BEAUTIFUL FRAGRANT FLOWERS THAT EMERGE FROM THE WATER. THEY FEATURE ABOUT 20 LARGE DOUBLE PETALS, WITH SHADES OF COLOR FROM WHITE, YELLOW, PINK, AND RED.

Just 0.31 inches

THE SMALL WATER LENTIL HAS A SINGLE WIRE-SHAPED ROOT, JUST 0.31 IN (8 MM) LONG.

164 ft

THE LENGTH KELP CAN REACH: IT IS A GIANT SEAWEED THAT FORMS UNDERWATER FORESTS AND PROVIDES FOOD AND HABITAT FOR VARIOUS OCEAN SPECIES, INCLUDING SEA OTTERS AND SEA LIONS.

THE STRUCTURE OF TREES

Trees are organisms of the plant kingdom also referred to as woody plants because...

...they possess a woody central body, the trunk, covered by a bark that protects it. From the trunk extend branches that carry leaves, forming the crown. At the base of the trunk are the roots that grow underground, anchor the tree to the ground, and absorb the necessary water and nutrients.

HOW OLD are you?

AS IT GROWS, THE TREE PRODUCES NEW WOOD AROUND OLD WOOD. GROWTH RINGS ARE THUS FORMED, WHICH CAN TELL THE AGE OF THE TREE.

400 BILLION

THE NUMBER OF TREES THAT ARE THOUGHT TO LIVE IN THE AMAZON RAINFOREST. BUT UNFORTUNATELY HUMANS ARE DOING A LOT OF DAMAGE, CUTTING DOWN LARGE AREAS OF THE FOREST EVERY YEAR!

A unique SHAPE!

EACH SPECIES HAS ITS OWN DISTINCTIVE ONE, BASED ON THE SHAPE OF THE FOLIAGE, WHICH ALLOWS US TO RECOGNIZE IT EVEN FROM A DISTANCE.

HONEYBERRY

IT IS A SLOW-GROWING, LONG-LIVED TREE: THAT IS, IT CAN LIVE FOR A LONG TIME, AND IT IS NOT DIFFICULT TO FIND CENTURY-OLD SPECIMENS!

200 MILION years ago

GINGKO BILOBA IS ONE OF THE OLDEST TREE SPECIES IN THE WORLD. IT HAS EXISTED FOR MORE THAN 200 MILLION YEARS AND SURVIVED THE DINOSAUR EXTINCTION. THEREFORE, WE CAN RIGHTFULLY CONSIDER IT A LIVING FOSSIL!

A delicious BARK

HAVE YOU EVER TASTED A CINNAMON PASTRY? THIS FRAGRANT SPICE IS NOTHING MORE THAN THE BARK OF THE TREE WITH THE SAME NAME.

Like a RAINBOW

RAINBOW EUCALYPTUS IS A TREE COMMON IN SOUTHEAST ASIA. IT GETS ITS NAME FROM ITS DISTINCTIVE BARK, WHICH SPLITS INTO MANY STRIPES AND IS COLORED PURPLE, RED, GREEN, BLUE, AND ORANGE.

2,000 liters

TREES CANNOT LIVE WITHOUT WATER. SOME SPECIES ACTUALLY ABSORB A LOT OF IT! A GIANT SEQUOIA CAN DRINK ALMOST 2,000 LITERS OF WATER A DAY.

FLOWERS

Thanks to flowers, it is possible to ensure the emergence of new seedlings.

The scent and color of flowers are "tricks" used by the plant to attract the insects responsible for its pollination. This fundamental process initiates the production of the fruit and seeds.

BLECH!

NOT ALL FLOWERS SMELL GOOD. THE HUGE TITAN ARUM, OR CORPSE FLOWER *(AMORPHOPHALLUS TITANUM)*, SMELLS LIKE ROTTING FLESH! THIS SMELL ATTRACTS THE FLIES THAT WILL POLLINATE THE PLANT.

IS IT A FLOWER OR NOT?

IF SOMEONE ASKED YOU TO DRAW A FLOWER YOU MIGHT THINK OF A DAISY, WHICH, HOWEVER, IS NOT ACTUALLY A FLOWER, BUT A COLLECTION OF NUMEROUS YELLOW MINI-FLOWERS FORMING THE CENTRAL DISK. SURROUNDING THIS IS A ROW OF WHITE FLOWERS WHOSE PETALS ARE FUSED INTO A SINGLE ELONGATED STRUCTURE.

THE BIRD OF PARADISE

THIS BEAUTIFUL SOUTH AFRICAN PLANT IS CALLED THE BIRD OF PARADISE BECAUSE OF ITS DISTINCTIVE SHAPE THAT RESEMBLES A HERON.

PARTS OF A FLOWER

GENERALLY, A FLOWER CONSISTS OF A CALYX, MADE UP OF THE SEPALS, SURROUNDING THE COROLLA FORMED BY THE PETALS. UNLIKE THE SEPALS, WHICH ARE GREEN, THE PETALS ARE OFTEN VERY COLORFUL. THEY PROTECT THE IMPORTANT ORGANS OF REPRODUCTION: THE MALE ONES, THE STAMENS, PRODUCE POLLEN, AND THE FEMALE ONES CONSIST OF THE PISTIL, IN WHOSE OVULES THE FRUIT WILL DEVELOP.

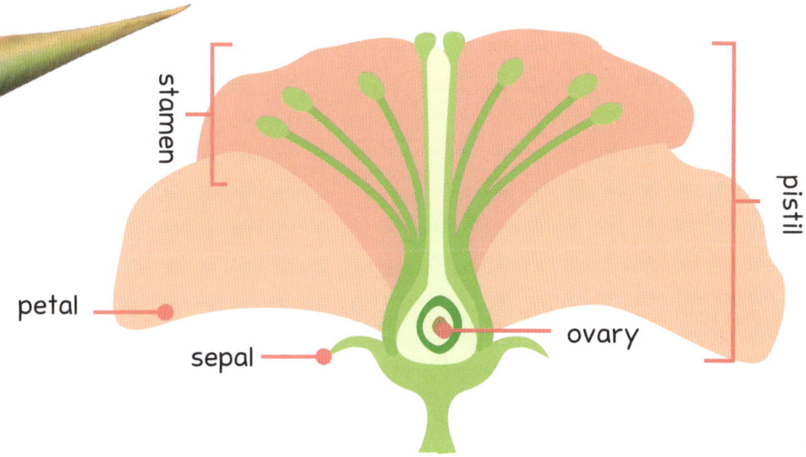

140 MILLION years ago

FLOWERS HAVE NOT EXISTED FOREVER; THEY FIRST APPEARED 140 MILLION YEARS AGO. BEFORE THEN, PLANTS SUCH AS FERNS AND CONIFERS, WHICH DO NOT FLOWER, DOMINATED EARTH.

FOUR o'clocks

THIS FLOWER'S BLOOMS OPEN AT DUSK, GIVING OFF A VERY INTENSE SCENT THAT ATTRACTS MOTHS.

The BIGGEST

THE *RAFFLESIA ARNOLDII* PLANT FROM THE RAINFORESTS OF INDONESIA PRODUCES A HUGE FLOWER THAT IS 3.28 FT (1 M) WIDE AND WEIGHS 22 LB (10 KG).

Thanks to the BUGS!

POLLINATION OF 90 PERCENT OF WILD FLOWERING SPECIES IS MAINLY DONE BY INSECTS; WITHOUT THEM, THE PLANTS WOULD NOT SURVIVE!

FRUITS

There are numerous and incredible varieties! Let's discover some!

Fruits are formed by the transformation of the ovary in flowering plants and are the part of the plant that contains the seeds. In addition to protecting and nourishing the valuable seed content, the fruit also promotes its dispersal in the seed environment.

352 lb

THIS IS THE INCREDIBLE WEIGHT ACHIEVED BY A WATERMELON SPECIMEN THAT WAS DEFINITELY ONE OF THE HEAVIEST FRUITS TO EVER EXIST!

APRICOT

Ancient FRUITS

THE DATE PALM HAS BEEN CULTIVATED FOR THOUSANDS OF YEARS, WHILE THE APRICOT TREE WAS INITIALLY GROWN IN CHINA "ONLY" 4,000 YEARS AGO.

STRAWBERRY medicine

THE EARLIEST INFORMATION ABOUT STRAWBERRIES IS FOUND IN ANCIENT TEXTS FROM THE 1500S, IN WHICH MONKS LISTED THE MANY USES OF THIS SMALL FRUIT AS MEDICINE.

VITAMIN C

VITAMINS ARE ESSENTIAL SUBSTANCES FOR OUR BODIES! VITAMIN C, FOR EXAMPLE, IS NEEDED TO HELP OUR IMMUNE SYSTEM. A QUICK WAY TO STOCK UP ON IT? EAT CITRUS FRUITS SUCH AS ORANGES, TANGERINES AND, ESPECIALLY, LEMONS.

The LARGEST SEED in the world

IS THAT OF THE SEA COCONUT PALM. IT IS PRODUCED WITHIN A FRUIT THAT TAKES AS LONG AS 10 YEARS TO RIPEN.

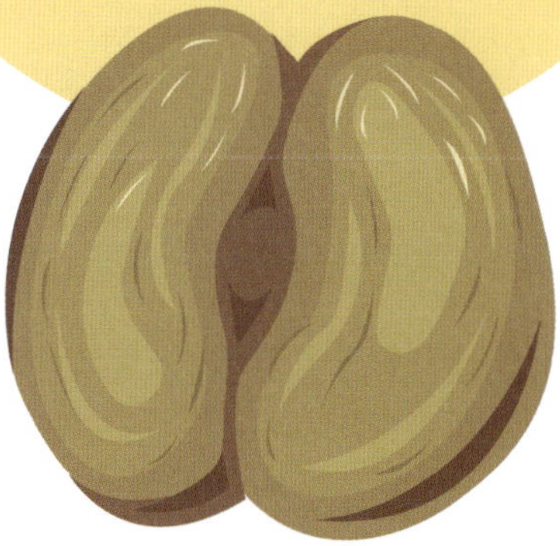

19.69 IN (50 CM)

WHAT A SMELL!

AMONG THE STRANGEST FRUITS IS CERTAINLY THE DURIAN, A LARGE, SPINY-SKINNED FRUIT, BEST KNOWN FOR ITS VERY PUNGENT SMELL THAT SOME FIND REVOLTING. FOR THIS REASON, IN SOUTHEAST ASIA IT IS FORBIDDEN TO BRING IT INTO PUBLIC PLACES OR EVEN TO KEEP IT IN HOTELS.

4,000 years ago

SOME FRUITS ARE THE PRODUCT OF A CROSS BETWEEN SPECIES. SUCH IS THE CASE WITH THE ORANGE, WHICH IS A HYBRID BORN MORE THAN 4,000 YEARS AGO FROM THE UNION OF A MANDARIN AND A POMELO.

PEACH

IT IS A FLESHY, JUICY, AND SUGARY FRUIT WITH A REDDISH-YELLOW SKIN THAT CAN BE THIN AND VELVETY OR SMOOTH.

MUSHROOMS

They are not plants or animals, but belong to a realm of their own.

The shape that immediately comes to mind when thinking of mushrooms is a stem topped by a cap, which can be of various sizes and colors, but the world of mushrooms is much broader!

In the DESERT?

WATER IS ESSENTIAL FOR FUNGI, BUT THERE ARE SOME THAT CAN SURVIVE EVEN AMONG THE SANDS OF THE DESERT, AN ENVIRONMENT THAT AT FIRST GLANCE WOULD SEEM TOO ARID FOR THE LIFE OF ANY ORGANISM.

MORTAL danger!

SOME MUSHROOMS CAN BE COOKED, BUT OTHERS ARE POISONOUS AND SOMETIMES DEADLY, SO DON'T PICK THEM WITHOUT KNOWING THEM THOROUGHLY!

SPOROPHORES

WHAT WE SEE POKING OUT OF THE GROUND ARE THE SPOROPHORES-THAT IS, THE FRUITS OF THE MUSHROOMS, WHICH DO NOT ALWAYS HAVE THE CLASSIC UMBRELLA SHAPE! IN MANY CASES THEIR APPEARANCE CAN BE SO STRANGE THAT THEY DO NOT EVEN LOOK LIKE MUSHROOMS.

WHAT IS UNDERNEATH?

IT SOUNDS STRANGE, BUT THE MOST IMPORTANT PART OF THE FUNGUS IS THE MYCELIUM THAT GROWS UNDERGROUND. IT CONSISTS OF A TANGLED WEB OF MILLIONS OF VERY THIN FILAMENTS, THE HYPHAE, WHICH ABSORB WATER AND NUTRIENTS FROM THE SOIL.

BIOLUMINESCENCE

SOME FUNGI, SUCH AS THE BLEEDING FAIRY HELMET, ARE BIOLUMINESCENT–THAT IS, THEY EMIT LIGHT IN THE DARK DUE TO PARTICULARY CHEMICAL REACTIONS.

3.86 miles²

THIS IS THE SURFACE AREA, EQUAL TO 1,350 FOOTBALL FIELDS, THAT IS COVERED BY THE FUNGUS *ARMILLARIA OSTOYAE*. IT IS THE LARGEST LIVING ORGANISM ON THE PLANET, AND WAS DISCOVERED IN 1998 IN OREGON.

SPORES

TO REPRODUCE, A FUNGUS PRODUCES MILLIONS OF TINY PARTICLES CALLED SPORES THAT ARE RELEASED TO GIVE RISE TO A NEW MYCELIUM WHEREVER THEY ARE DEPOSITED.

CEP

IT IS A FUNGUS WIDELY USED IN COOKING THAT GROWS IN THE WOODS, NEAR OAK, CHESTNUT, BEECH, AND CONIFER TREES.

LEAVES

They are one of the most important parts of a plant.

Leaves are indispensable because it is within them that a very important chemical reaction-photosynthesis-takes place, which enables the plant to grow.

Around 200,000

THE NUMBER VARIES ON THE TYPE OF LEAF, BUT THE CROWN OF A LARGE, ADULT TREE CAN EASILY EXCEED 200,000 LEAVES!

3x2

LEAVES VARY GREATLY IN SIZE, SHAPE, AND COLOR, BUT MOST HAVE A WIDE, FLAT AREA CALLED THE LAMINA. THE GIANT TARO HAS THE LARGEST LAMINA OF ALL: MORE THAN 3 METERS (9.8 FT) LONG AND 2 METERS (6.5 FT) WIDE.

The BIGGEST ones!

THE LEAVES OF THE RAFFIA PALM CAN REACH A LENGTH OF 82 FT (25 M), WHICH IS AS TALL AS A SEVEN-STORY BUILDING, AND WEIGH AS MUCH AS 880 LB (400 KG)! THIS PLANT HOLDS THE RECORD AS THE SPECIES WITH THE LARGEST LEAVES IN THE WORLD.

VEINS

THE LEAF IS CRISSCROSSED BY "CHANNELS" CALLED VEINS. LIKE OUR VEINS, THEY CARRY NUTRIENTS PRODUCED BY THE LEAVES TO THE REST OF THE TREE AND CARRY WATER AND MINERALS FROM THE ROOTS TO THE LEAVES.

CHLOROPHYLL

THE GREEN COLORATION OF LEAVES DEPENDS ON THE PRESENCE OF CHLOROPHYLL, A PIGMENT SO VALUABLE THAT EVERY SINGLE DROP MUST BE PRESERVED. THEREFORE, BEFORE THE LEAF FALLS OFF, THE CHLOROPHYLL IS "DISASSEMBLED" INTO SMALL PARTS THAT ARE MOVED AND STORED WITHIN THE BRANCHES AND STEM. THE LEAF THEN CHANGES COLOR.

All DIFFERENT!

IN THE BLACK MULBERRY, THE LEAVES ARE ALL DIFFERENT, EVEN ON THE SAME BRANCH. THIS TRULY BIZARRE FEATURE DOES NOT SEEM TO HAVE A SPECIFIC PURPOSE.

PHILODENDRON LEAVES

ITS NAME IS OF GREEK ORIGIN AND MEANS "HE WHO LOVES THE TREE," AN EXPRESSION THAT INDICATES HOW THE PHILODENDRON CLIMBS BY "EMBRACING" THE TREE AROUND WHICH IT GROWS.

Many FORMS

LEAVES MAY BE ROUND, OVAL, LANCE-SHAPED, HEART-SHAPED, OR TRIANGULAR, WITH SMOOTH OR SERRATED EDGES, WHILE OTHERS ARE THIN, LIKE NEEDLES.

CONIFERS

The word "conifer" is derived from Latin and means "cone-bearer."

This is how those trees and shrubs that bear cones on their branches got their name. In the male cones, pollen is produced, while in the female cones, seeds are found.

550

THERE ARE MORE THAN 550 TYPES OF CONIFERS; SOME OF THE BEST KNOWN ARE:

CEDARS, CYPRESSES, FIRS, JUNIPERS, LARCHES, PINES, REDWOODS, AND YEWS.

NEEDLES

THE LEAVES OF CONIFERS ARE VERY THIN, AND BECAUSE OF THEIR APPEARANCE, THEY ARE CALLED NEEDLES; THESE PLANTS ARE ALSO KNOWN AS NEEDLE TREES. GENERALLY THE NEEDLES APPEAR ON THE BRANCHES IN BUNCHES OR IN ROWS. IN SPECIES LIVING IN COLD REGIONS THEY ARE NO MORE THAN 2.36 IN (6 CM) LONG, WHILE THEY ARE UP TO 7.87 IN (20 CM) LONG IN THOSE ADAPTED TO MILDER CLIMATES.

LARGE and small

CONIFERS ARE AMONG THE TALLEST AND HEAVIEST LIVING THINGS ON EARTH, BUT THERE ARE ALSO VERY SMALL ONES. GARDENERS HAVE SELECTED SOME DWARF VARIETIES THAT ARE NO TALLER THAN 19.69 IN (50 CM).

EVERGREENS

MOST CONIFERS ARE EVERGREEN TREES BECAUSE THE BRANCHES RETAIN THEIR LEAVES ALL YEAR ROUND, REPLACING THEM ON A CONTINUOUS CYCLE.

PINE NUTS

WHEN A PINE CONE RECEIVES WIND-BLOWN POLLEN, SEED PRODUCTION BEGINS UNDER THE SCALES. WHEN THE SEEDS ARE RIPE, THE SCALES OPEN, LETTING THEM FALL TO THE GROUND.

11 lb

THE RECORD WEIGHT OF A CONE OF THE COULTER PINE!

40 MILLION years ago

IN 1994, AN AUSTRALIAN RANGER DISCOVERED A GROUP OF CENTURIES-OLD TREES HE HAD NEVER SEEN BEFORE, IN A REMOTE CANYON IN WOLLEMI NATIONAL PARK. IT WAS A NEWLY DISCOVERED SPECIES AND WAS GIVEN THE NAME OF THE PARK: THE WOLLEMI PINE. VERY RARE TODAY, IT WAS COMMON THROUGHOUT AUSTRALIA 40 MILLION YEARS AGO.

THE PINE CONES

ALTHOUGH VERY DIFFERENT FROM EACH OTHER, DEPENDING ON THE SPECIES, IN SHAPE AND COLOR, ALL PINE CONES ARE ACCOMULATED BY THE SCALES THAT INITIALLY PROTECT THE SEED, AND THEN DROP IT BY OPENING, UPON MATURATION.

PHOTOSYNTHESIS

This activity produces oxygen as a waste substance, which is released into the air.

Photosynthesis is a complex process that takes place in leaves to transform the sun's energy into a sugar, called glucose, that is the plant's main nutrient.

CELL OF A PLANT

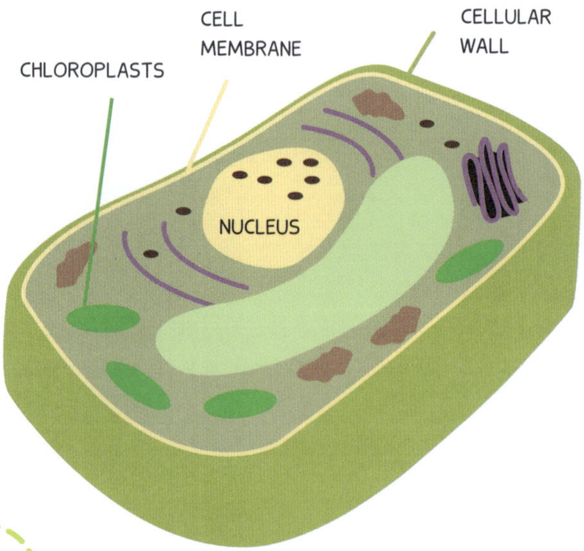

2.5 BILLION years ago

THE FIRST ORGANISMS TO USE PHOTOSYNTHESIS AND FILL THE ATMOSPHERE WITH OXYGEN WERE SOME SPECIAL MARINE BACTERIA MORE THAN 2.5 BILLION YEARS AGO.

INGREDIENTS

WATER NEEDED FOR PHOTOSYNTHESIS IS ABSORBED FROM THE SOIL THROUGH THE ROOTS, WHILE CARBON DIOXIDE ENTERS THE LEAVES DIRECTLY FROM THE AIR. THE LAST, CRUCIAL INGREDIENT IS SUNLIGHT.

CHLOROPLASTS

WITHIN THE LEAF, CHLOROPHYLL IS COLLECTED WITHIN SMALL ORGANELLES, THE CHLOROPLASTS. A SINGLE PLANT CELL CONTAINS 20 TO 100 CHLOROPLASTS, SO WE CAN EXPECT TO FIND ABOUT HALF A MILLION OF THEM IN EACH SQUARE MILLIMETER IN A LEAF.

The RECIPE

PHOTOSYNTHESIS OCCURS IN LEAVES, WHERE CHLOROPHYLL COMBINES WATER, THANKS TO ENERGY GAINED FROM THE SUN'S RAYS, WITH CARBON DIOXIDE, PRODUCING GLUCOSE.

1771

IN 1771, ENGLISH SCIENTIST JOSEPH PRIESTLEY BEGAN STUDYING PHOTOSYNTHESIS ON A SPRIG OF MINT AND WAS THE FIRST TO NOTICE THAT WHEN PLACED IN SUNLIGHT, PLANTS PRODUCE A GAS, LATER IDENTIFIED AS OXYGEN.

GLUCOSE

GLUCOSE CAN BE DISTRIBUTED THROUGHOUT THE TREE AS NOURISHMENT, OR IT CAN BE USED TO CREATE PRECISE PARTS OF IT, SUCH AS FRUIT, WHOSE SWEET TASTE DEPENDS ON THE PRESENCE OF THIS SUGAR!

1,200,000 gigatonnes

IT HAS BEEN ESTIMATED THAT THERE ARE 1,200,000 GIGATONNES (OR BILLIONS OF TONS) OF OXYGEN IN THE ATMOSPHERE TODAY, ALMOST ENTIRELY PRODUCED BY PHOTOSYNTHESIS OF BOTH MARINE PLANTS, SUCH AS ALGAE, AND TERRESTRIAL PLANTS.

SUCCULENT PLANTS

The botanical name is derived from the latin word for "juice."

They are plants that store water by impregnating particular spongy tissues in the stem and leaves, which is why they appear juicy.

10,000

THE NUMBER OF SPECIES OF SUCCULENT PLANTS, WHICH ARE DIVIDED INTO 60 FAMILIES, INCLUDING THE CACTUS FAMILY.

The BIGGEST!

CACTI CAN BE AS SMALL AS ROCKS OR VERY LARGE. THE SAGUARO IS THE LARGEST CACTUS IN NORTH AMERICA AND CAN EASILY EXCEED 32 FT (10 M) IN HEIGHT.

HURRY UP!

SOME SPECIES PRODUCE FLOWERS OF EXTRAORDINARY BEAUTY IN SHAPE AND COLOR. UNFORTUNATELY, VERY OFTEN THERE IS NOT ENOUGH TIME TO ADMIRE THEM BECAUSE THEY BLOOM AND FADE OVERNIGHT.

SPINES or LEAVES?

IN CACTI, THE SPINES ARE NOTHING MORE THAN MODIFIED LEAVES, WHICH LIMIT TRANSPIRATION AND CONSEQUENT LOSS OF VALUABLE WATER.

Ancient CACTI

THE FIRST CACTI APPEARED BETWEEN 5 AND 10 MILLION YEARS AGO WHEN, AFTER A LONG PERIOD OF DROUGHT, EARTH'S CLIMATE WAS PERFECT FOR THEIR GROWTH.

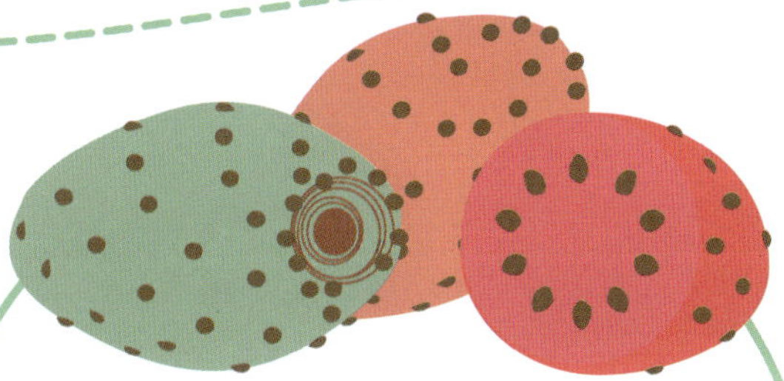

More than 300...

THE NUMBER OF SEEDS CONTAINED IN EACH PRICKLY PEAR, A FRUIT THAT IS DIFFICULT TO EAT BECAUSE IT IS COVERED WITH A THICK, THORNY SKIN.

AGAVE

THE 100-YEAR-OLD AGAVE TAKES UP TO 50 YEARS TO MAKE ITS FLOWERS, WHICH ARE BORNE BY A STEM UP TO 30 FT (9 M) TALL. THIS TAKES GREAT EFFORT BY THE PLANT, WHICH SOON FADES AND DIES.

HOT and COLD

SUCCULENT PLANTS DO NOT ONLY LIVE WHERE IT IS VERY HOT; SOME SPECIES IN SOUTH AMERICA HAVE ADAPTED TO LIVE IN COLD TEMPERATURES, AS LOW AS 32°F (0°C).

ECHEVERIA

THE NAME IS A TRIBUTE TO THE MEXICAN PAINTER ATANASIO ECHEVERRÍA, FAMOUS FOR HIS PLANT PAINTINGS. THIS SUCCULENT HAS FLAT, FLESHY LEAVES ARRANGED IN A ROSETTE.

CARNIVOROUS PLANTS

Usually it is plants that are eaten by animals, but there are exceptions...

Some plants have reversed roles and feed on insects and other small animals. These meals represent a "snack," because in reality, as with all green plants, the main source of food always comes from photosynthesis caused by sunlight.

GENLISEA

THE GENLISEA HAS PARTS OF THE LEAVES RESEMBLING DOWNWARD-FACING TUBULES. THESE FORCE PREY TO ADVANCE DEEPER INTO THE LAST CHAMBER, WHERE THEY WILL BE DIGESTED.

DIONEA

THE VENUS FLYTRAP HAS A SNAP TRAP. THE LEAVES CLOSE WHEN AN ANIMAL INADVERTENTLY TOUCHES THE THIN SENSITIVE HAIRS ON THE INNER SURFACE. THE PREY IS THEN TRAPPED INSIDE BY SPINY "TEETH" PRESENT ON THE EDGE.

630

THE NUMBER OF CARNIVOROUS PLANT SPECIES WORLDWIDE. HOWEVER, MANY ARE FACING EXTINCTION DUE TO CLIMATE CHANGE.

5 traps

CATCHING A MOVING ANIMAL FOR THOSE ANCHORED TO THE GROUND IS CERTAINLY NOT EASY. THEREFORE, CARNIVOROUS PLANTS HAVE DEVELOPED DIFFERENT TYPES OF TRAPS: SNAP, DROP, STICKY, SUCTION, AND DEAD-END.

Delicious POOP

SOME SPECIES OF NEPENTHES EAT EXCREMENT! THE PLANT ATTRACTS THE TUPAIA, A SMALL ASIAN MAMMAL, WITH SUGARY SUBSTANCES. WHILE FEEDING, THE TUPAIA POOPS INSIDE THE OPENING OF THE PLANT.

Good FLOWERS

CARNIVOROUS PLANTS MUST SEPARATE PREY FROM POLLINATING INSECTS, WHICH ARE A VALUABLE AID TO THEIR REPRODUCTION. THUS, THEY GROW "TRUE" FLOWERS AT THE ENDS OF LONG STEMS, MAKING THEM BLOOM AS FAR AS POSSIBLE FROM THEIR INVITING AND DEADLY TRAPS.

32.8 ft

THE HEIGHT THAT THE NEPENTHES RAJAH CAN REACH BY CLIMBING.

47 MILLION years ago

THE OLDEST FOSSIL OF A CARNIVOROUS PLANT *(RORIDULA)* WAS FOUND IN BALTIC AMBER AND DATES FROM 35 TO 47 MILLION YEARS AGO.

POISONOUS AND STINGING PLANTS

Some plants can be dangerous because they are rich in toxic substances.

They hide toxic substances in the fruits, seeds, or the whole plant that can irritate the skin or even be poisonous if ingested. Unlike animals, plants do not have the ability to escape, and with this secret weapon they protect themselves.

DANGER in the GARDEN...

MANY PLANTS GROWN IN GARDENS HIDE AN UNSUSPECTED DANGER. OLEANDER, FOR EXAMPLE, CAUSE NAUSEA AND VOMITING, AND NARCISSUS HAS A LETHAL BULB.

...and in the KITCHEN

THE SOLANACEAE IS A STRANGE PLANT FAMILY: IT INCLUDES SPECIES WHOSE FRUITS WE EAT, SUCH AS THE TOMATO AND EGGPLANT, BUT ALSO OTHERS THAT ARE VERY TOXIC, SUCH AS THE NIGHTSHADE, WHOSE BERRIES ARE EXTREMELY POISONOUS.

Delicate but POISONOUS!

IN THE LANGUAGE OF FLOWERS, LILY OF THE VALLEY IS THE SYMBOL OF LOVE, BUT THE HIGH CONCENTRATION OF TOXINS IN THE WHITE FLOWERS AND RED BERRIES MAKE IT VERY DANGEROUS!

It STINGS!

THE TERRIBLE NETTLE IS COVERED WITH HAIRS WITH SILICA TIPS THAT RELEASE STINGING MOLECULES ON OUR SKIN, MAKING THE PAIN PROLONGED.

A giant NOT to be TOUCHED!

THE AUSTRALIAN *DENDROCNID MOROIDES* IS UP TO 10 FT (3 M) TALL AND IS ENTIRELY COVERED WITH STINGING HAIRS. TOUCHING THE STEM OR THE LARGE HEART-SHAPED LEAVES CAUSES A VERY STRONG BURNING SENSATION THAT CAN LAST UP TO TWO DAYS.

Toxic KERNELS

POISON CAN ALSO BE FOUND WHERE YOU LEAST EXPECT IT: THE SEEDS AND KERNELS OF MANY TASTY FRUITS CONTAIN CYANIDE, A POISON THAT HAS A BAD REPUTATION BECAUSE IT IS OFTEN USED TO CARRY OUT CRIMES IN MYSTERY BOOKS.

DEADLY NIGHTSHADE

POPULAR BELIEF HELD THAT THIS MOST POISONOUS SPECIES WAS THE MAIN INGREDIENT USED TO MAKE DEADLY POTIONS BY WITCHES AND SORCERERS.

KITCHEN GARDEN

There is a diverse group of plants that are very important in human nutrition.

They are a source of energy and contain vitamins, fiber, water, and minerals that enable us to live a healthy life!

20,000

THE NUMBER OF EDIBLE PLANTS THAT WE MIGHT EAT, INCLUDING THE FRUITS, THE FLOWERS, THE SEEDS, THE LEAVES, THE TUBERS, AND THE BULBS.

Space POTATOES

THE FIRST VEGETABLE TO BE GROWN IN SPACE WAS A POTATO. IN OCTOBER 1995 IT WAS GROWN ABOARD THE SPACE SHUTTLE COLUMBIA.

FRUITS or VEGETABLES?

ALTHOUGH WE DO NOT THINK OF THEM AS SUCH, TOMATOES, SQUASH, ZUCCHINI, AND CUCUMBERS ARE FRUITS AND STORE SEEDS WITHIN THEM.

Buds of BROCCOLI

BROCCOLI ARE THE LITTLE FLOWERS OF THE PLANT THAT HAVE NOT YET OPENED. THESE VEGETABLES CONTAIN MORE VITAMIN C THAN ORANGES!

TOMATO

IT IS NATIVE TO THE AMERICAS AND WAS CULTIVATED BY THE AZTECS AS EARLY AS 700 CE.

BEET

IN 2001, THE WORLD'S HEAVIEST BEET WAS HARVESTED: IT WEIGHED AN IMPRESSIVE 51.58 LB (23.4 KG).

Egyptian LETTUCE

THE ANCIENT EGYPTIANS WERE AMONG THE FIRST TO CULTIVATE LETTUCE, APPRECIATING IT FOR ITS SUCCULENT LEAVES. BEFORE IT WAS A FOOD, IT WAS CULTIVATED TO PRODUCE OIL FROM ITS SEEDS.

CARROTS

THE PART OF THE CARROT YOU EAT IS ACTUALLY THE ROOT OF THE PLANT!

THE CARROT WAS ORIGINALLY PURPLE, NOT ORANGE. ITS PRESENT COLOR IS THE RESULT OF BREEDING BY DUTCH FARMERS WHO WANTED TO PAY HOMAGE TO THEIR NATIONAL HERO, WILLIAM OF ORANGE.

AGRICULTURE

AROUND 10,000 BCE, AT THE END OF THE LAST ICE AGE, HUMANS BEGAN TO CULTIVATE SOME OF THE PLANTS THEY HAD PREVIOUSLY GATHERED WHEN MOVING FROM PLACE TO PLACE; THUS AGRICULTURE WAS BORN.

GREEN GIANTS

Here we'll discover the characteristics of some huge "living monuments."

It is known that every year trees grow a little bigger, but some species are programmed to reach a huge size over a time span of centuries or even millennia.

The GREATEST!

A GIANT SEQUOIA IN CALIFORNIA IS THE LARGEST TREE IN THE WORLD! IT IS CALLED GENERAL SHERMAN AND EXCEEDS 262.46 FT (80 M) IN HEIGHT, WHILE THE DIAMETER OF ITS TRUNK IS A WHOPPING 36 FT (11 M).

Among the FLOWERS

AMONG FLOWERING PLANTS, THE TITLE OF "GIANT" IS HELD BY THE AUSTRALIAN EUCALYPTUS. A SPECIMEN DISCOVERED IN 2008 IN TASMANIA HAS A HEIGHT OF NEARLY 328 FT (100 M).

The WIDEST FOLIAGE

THE CANOPY OF A BANYAN TREE CALLED THIMMAMMA MARRIMANU, CONSIDERED SACRED BY THE INDIAN PEOPLE, IS LARGER THAN TWO SOCCER FIELDS!

The GREAT HYPERION

SEQUOIA SEMPERVIRENS IS THE TALLEST TREE SPECIES IN THE WORLD. THE TALLEST SPECIMEN ON RECORD IS FOUND IN CALIFORNIA AND HAS BEEN NAMED HYPERION. IT EXCEEDS 377.29 FT (115 M).

A HUGE CACTUS!

CACTI ALSO HAVE THEIR MAXIMUM HEIGHT: ONE ELEPHANT CACTUS SPECIMEN WAS RECORDED AT MORE THAN 62.33 FT (19 M), DUE MAINLY TO THE LENGTH OF ITS BRANCHES.

Crazy DIAMETERS

NEW ZEALAND IS HOME TO KAURI *(AGATHIS AUSTRALIS)*, WHICH MEANS "LORDS OF THE FOREST" IN THE MAORI LANGUAGE. WITH A HEIGHT APPROACHING 164 FT (50 M) AND A DIAMETER OF MORE THAN 32.80 (10 M), THEY ARE TRULY IMPOSING TREES.

VISIT MEXICO IF YOU WANT TO SEE A MONTEZUMA CYPRESS WITH AN IMMENSE IRREGULAR TRUNK; IT HAS A CIRCUMFERENCE EXCEEDING 114.82 FT (35 M).

What a STUNNER!

WHEN THE DYERVILLE GIANT CRASHED TO THE GROUND IN 1991, THE IMPACT PRODUCED SUCH A LOUD NOISE THAT PEOPLE THOUGHT IT WAS A TRAIN COLLISION. THE GROUND VIBRATION WAS EVEN PICKED UP BY SEISMOGRAPHS. IT WAS A 360.89-FT TALL (110-M) *SEQUOIA SEMPERVIRENS*.

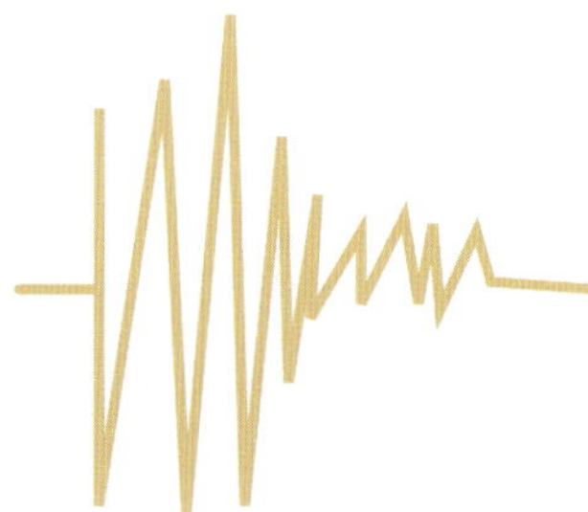

BAOBAB

THE AFRICAN BAOBAB, ALSO CALLED THE "TREE OF LIFE," IS A HUGE TREE OF THE SAVANNAS, REACHING 82 FT (25 M) IN HEIGHT AND 23 FT (7 M) IN DIAMETER.

CENTURIES-OLD PLANTS

The lifespan of plants varies greatly from that of animals!

Several plant species quietly reach the century mark, but others live much longer, longer than humans and probably almost any other living thing. In fact, they can cross the 1,000-year mark without showing much age at all.

Before the PYRAMIDS!

IN 1964 A BRISTLECONE PINE, KNOWN BY THE NICKNAME PROMETHEUS, WAS CUT DOWN IN NEVADA FOR RESEARCH PURPOSES, AND IT WAS FOUND TO BE MORE THAN 4,850 YEARS OLD. WHEN IT SPROUTED, THE OLDEST PYRAMIDS HAD NOT YET BEEN BUILT.

OAK

A VERY LONG-LIVED TREE. IT USUALLY REACHES 200 YEARS OLD, BUT SOME SPECIMENS LIVE MORE THAN A THOUSAND YEARS!

Thousand-year-old TREE

THERE IS A CYPRESS TREE LOCATED IN IRAN THAT IS ESTIMATED TO BE AT LEAST 4,000 YEARS OLD, AND IT IS CONSIDERED A NATIONAL MONUMENT.

The prehistoric YEW

IN WALES, UNITED KINGDOM, LIVES A YEW TREE IN EXCELLENT HEALTH, NOTWITHSTANDING ITS AGE OF ABOUT 4,000 YEARS. WHEN IT STARTED GROWING THE LOCAL PEOPLE WERE STILL LIVING IN THE BRONZE AGE!

PATAGONIA'S great-grandfather

THIS IS THE NICKNAME GIVEN TO A PATAGONIAN CYPRESS TREE IN CHILE. IN 2022 AN ENVIRONMENTAL SCIENTIST ESTIMATED ITS VENERABLE AGE AT 4,853 YEARS.

A legendary CHESTNUT TREE

THE OLDEST KNOWN CHESTNUT TREE IN THE WORLD IS ABOUT 3,000 YEARS OLD AND IS LOCATED IN ITALY. IT IS CALLED THE HUNDRED HORSES CHESTNUT BECAUSE, ACCORDING TO LEGEND, 100 HORSEMEN AND THEIR STEEDS FOUND SHELTER FROM A STORM UNDER ITS IMMENSE CANOPY.

The centuries-old OLIVE TREE

ON THE GREEK ISLAND OF CRETE, AN OLIVE TREE HAS BEEN PRODUCING HIGHLY PRIZED OLIVES EVERY YEAR FOR AT LEAST 2,000 YEARS.

TRAVELING SEEDS

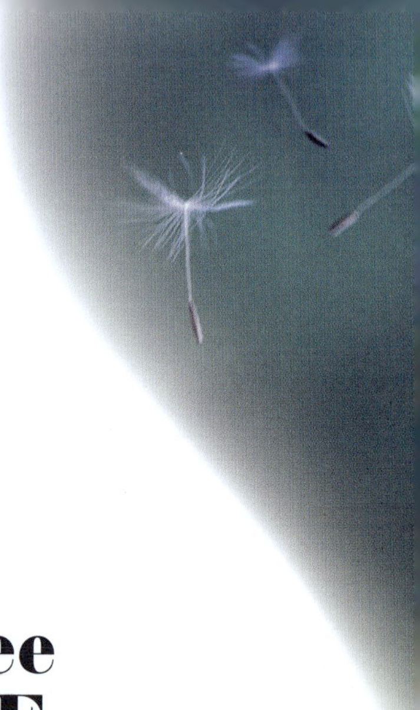

After producing seeds, a plant's task is not yet finished.

It must, in fact, make sure that its seeds are dispersed, preferably a little far away, so that the new seedlings can find an uncrowded place to grow. The modes of dispersal can be quite incredible.

A Free RIDE

THIS IS THE METHOD USED BY MANY SEEDS EQUIPPED WITH A STICKY, SPINY, OR HOOKED COATING. THEY HARPOON THEMSELVES TO THE FEATHERS OR FUR OF ANIMALS, THUS MOVING AWAY FROM THEIR PLACE OF ORIGIN.

Relying on THE WAVES

COCONUT PALMS HAVE LARGE, HEFTY SEEDS THAT ARE CONTAINED IN A LIGHTWEIGHT SHELL THAT ALLOWS THEM TO FLOAT. THEY ARE RELEASED INTO THE SEA SO THAT THE WAVES PUSH THEM TO OTHER ISLANDS.

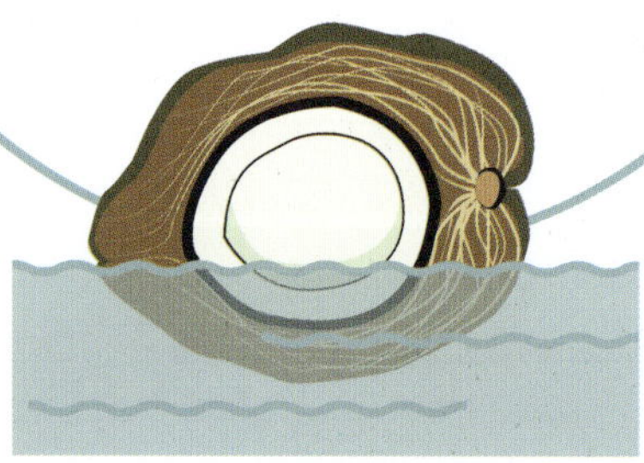

Explosive SEEDS!

SOMETIMES SEEDS ARE RELEASED IN AN EXPLOSION! AT A MERE TOUCH, THE GERANIUM BLASTS OUT ITS SEEDS, HURLING THEM IN ALL DIRECTIONS, WITH THE INTENTION THAT THEY WILL LAND ON FERTILE SOIL.

Mission: POOP!

SOME SEEDS PRODUCED WITHIN DELICIOUS FRUIT EXPLOIT A "PASSAGEWAY"! AFTER THE FRUIT HAS BEEN EATEN BY AN ANIMAL, THE SEEDS PASS THROUGH ITS INTESTINES INTACT AND RETURN TO THE SOIL THROUGH THE DROPPINGS. IT'S ALSO A GREAT WAY TO GUARANTEE A NICE BIT OF FERTILIZER!

DANDELION

AIR CAN ALSO BE A MEANS OF TRANSPORT: IN THE DANDELION THE SEED IS EQUIPPED WITH A MINI-PARACHUTE MADE OF BRISTLES CALLED THE PAPPUS, WHICH FACILITATES ITS MOVEMENT BY THE WIND.

In free FALL

TREES LIKE THE WALNUT OR APPLE TAKE ADVANTAGE OF GRAVITY; AS THEY REACH MATURITY, THE FRUIT CONTAINING THE SEEDS FALLS TO THE GROUND AS THE STALK SPLITS FROM THE BRANCH.

Winged SEEDS

THESE ARE CHARACTERISTIC OF SOME PLANTS SUCH AS THE MAPLE TREE. THEIR SEED IS JOINED TO A SMALL HELIX-LIKE STRUCTURE. WHEN IT FALLS, THE PROPELLER PRODUCES A SPIRAL MOTION THAT CARRIES IT AWAY FROM THE TREE.

HANGING PLANTS

Plants often take strange forms to survive.

Some, for example, choose to lean against another plant, a pole, or a rock to reach the sun's rays and use their roots only to hold themselves in place. These are the epiphytes. Other species, such as climbers, have roots in the ground but grow by climbing up other plants or vertical structures.

Aerial PLANTS

THIS IS THE OTHER NAME BY WHICH EPIPHYTES ARE KNOWN. IN FACT, THE ROOTS OF THESE PLANTS DO NOT PUSH INTO THE SOIL BUT OBTAIN MOISTURE AND NUTRIENTS FROM THE ENVIRONMENT OR AIR.

One big FAMILY

MOST EPIPHYTES ARE FLOWERING PLANTS, SUCH AS THE BEAUTIFUL ORCHIDS WHOSE FAMILY, CONSISTING OF MORE THAN 25,000 SPECIES, IS AMONG THE LARGEST IN THE PLANT KINGDOM.

VANILLA IS ALSO AN ORCHID! FROM ITS PODS, WHICH ARE ITS FRUIT, THE DELICATE SPICE OF THE SAME NAME THAT IS WIDELY USED IN SWEETS IS MADE.

VANILLA PODS

A weak STEM

THE VINE STEM IS TOO WEAK TO GROW UPRIGHT WITHOUT SUPPORT. IN NATURE, VINES CRAWL ON THE GROUND OR USE PLANTS, ROCKS, AND OTHER STRUCTURES, TO WHICH THEY ATTACH THEMSELVES THROUGH TENDRILS, AS SUPPORT.

Intrusive LIANAS

CLIMBING PLANTS INCLUDE LIANAS, WHICH ARE WIDESPREAD IN TROPICAL FORESTS. ONCE THEY REACH THE CANOPY OF THE PLANT ON WHICH THEY HAVE CLIMBED, THEY ARE ABLE TO CONTINUE THEIR GROWTH BY SPREADING FROM TREE TO TREE.

IVY

IVY IS A CLIMBING PLANT. IT CLIMBS UP OTHER PLANTS OR STRUCTURES BY USING SMALL ROOTS THAT LATCH ONTO EACH HANDHOLD.

A tadpole POOL

BROMELIADS CAN COLLECT LARGE AMOUNTS OF WATER BETWEEN THEIR ROSETTE LEAVES. BECAUSE OF THIS CHARACTERISTIC, IN THE FOREST THEY OFTEN SERVE AS A "POOL" FOR THE TADPOLES OF SOME SPECIES OF SMALL TROPICAL FROGS.

Looks can be DECEIVING!

TYPICALLY AN EPIPHYTE GROWS SLOWLY, AND IN SOME YEARS IT MAY NOT EVEN GROW AT ALL! THIS MEANS THAT EVEN VERY SMALL SEEDLINGS CAN ACTUALLY BE MANY YEARS OLD.

WOOD WIDE WEB

Plants have developed a symbiotic relationship with fungi for communication.

Indeed, underneath every forest is a complex secret network of roots, fungi, and bacteria that carries information and, according to some scientists, even nutrients, linking plants together.

Like the INTERNET

THE FIRST PERSON TO TALK ABOUT THE "WOOD WIDE WEB" WAS THE AMERICAN SCIENTIST SUZANNE SIMARD WHO, NOTING MANY SIMILARITIES BETWEEN THE TWO FORMS OF COMMUNICATION, CHOSE A NAME REMINISCENT OF THE INTERNET'S INFORMATION NETWORK.

Messenger MUSHROOMS

THIS SECRET SOCIAL NETWORK BETWEEN FUNGI AND PLANTS HAS BEEN ACTIVE FOR NEARLY 500 MILLION YEARS. FUNGI ARE RESPONSIBLE FOR SORTING AND TRANSMITTING ALL INFORMATION FROM ONE TREE TO ANOTHER.

Important INFORMATION!

A WOOD WIDE WEB ALLOWS ALL TREES TO HAVE UNDERGROUND CONVERSATIONS, FOR EXAMPLE, ISSUING WARNINGS ABOUT AN IMPENDING PEST ATTACK, OR AN ONGOING STATE OF DROUGHT, OR THE SPREAD OF A DISEASE.

Equal EXCHANGE

FROM THIS COLLABORATION THE TREES OBTAIN VALUABLE NUTRIENTS, SUCH AS NITROGEN AND PHOSPHORUS, WHICH THE FUNGI ASSIMILATE FROM THE SOIL, AND IN RETURN THE FUNGI RECEIVE CARBON-RICH SUGAR NUTRIENTS FROM TREE ROOTS.

A huge NETWORK

SCIENTISTS CALCULATE THAT ABOUT 90 PERCENT OF LAND PLANTS ARE CONNECTED TO EACH OTHER BY THIS UNDERGROUND JUNCTION OF LONG, THIN FILAMENTS.

MOTHER TREES

RESEARCH HAS DISCOVERED THE EXISTENCE OF "MOTHER" TREES, AMONG THE LARGEST AND OLDEST TREES IN THE FOREST. THEIR JOB IS TO BE A HUB OF NETWORKED INFORMATION, AND THEREFORE THEY ARE KEY ELEMENTS FOR ALL PLANT SPECIES PRESENT.

Plant MOMS

JUST AS A MOTHER WOULD, MOTHER PLANTS ESPECIALLY TAKE CARE OF THE YOUNGER AND WEAKER PLANTS, DISTRIBUTING THE NECESSARY RESOURCES TO THEM THROUGH THE NETWORK.

HERBACEOUS PLANTS

Instead of a trunk they have green, tender, and flexible stems.

Generally their life cycle is much shorter than that of woody plants, so they grow quickly and produce flowers and many seeds in a very short period of time.

More than 10,000

THE VARIETIES OF HERBACEOUS PLANTS, DIFFERENT IN SHAPE AND SIZE BUT WIDESPREAD IN ALMOST EVERY HABITAT ON OUR PLANET.

A short LIFE

MOST GRASSES LIVE ONLY ONE YEAR AND DIE AT THE END OF THE SUMMER SEASON DURING WHICH THEY PRODUCED FIRST FLOWERS, THEN FRUITS, AND FINALLY SEEDS, WHICH ARE DROPPED ON THE GROUND FOR NEW SEEDLINGS TO EMERGE IN THE SPRING.

Waiting for the WARMTH

IN SOME SPECIES, WITH THE COMING OF WINTER ONLY THE PART OF THE PLANT THAT SPROUTS FROM THE GROUND DIES. THE UNDERGROUND ROOTS ARE PRESERVED, AND FROM THESE THE PLANT WILL SPROUT AGAIN AS SOON AS THERE ARE SUITABLE ENVIRONMENTAL CONDITIONS TO DO SO.

The biggest GRASS

THE PUYA IS ALSO CALLED THE QUEEN OF THE ANDES BECAUSE IT IS NATIVE TO THE HIGH MOUNTAINS OF BOLIVIA AND PERU. ITS FLOWER IS A SPIKE THAT REACHES 33-39 FT (10-12 M) IN HEIGHT AND IS 7.8 FT (2.4 M) IN DIAMETER.

BAMBOO

FLEXIBLE BAMBOOS ARE VERY SPECIAL GRASSES. IN ADDITION TO HAVING VERY RAPID GROWTH THEY HOLD A FASCINATING SECRET: THEY FLOWER AT MYSTERIOUS INTERVALS, TYPICALLY RANGING FROM 65 TO 120 YEARS, AND INDIVIDUALS THAT COME FROM THE SAME MOTHER PLANT ALL DO SO AT THE SAME TIME, WHEREVER THEY ARE IN THE WORLD.

An unexpected GRASS

DESPITE THEIR SIZE, WHICH IS MUCH LARGER THAN THE COMMON GRASSES WE KNOW, AND THEIR TREE-LIKE APPEARANCE, BANANA PLANTS ARE CONSIDERED HERBACEOUS BECAUSE THEY HAVE NO WOODY PARTS.

RECORD-BREAKING PLANTS

Some plants surprise us with their outstanding characteristics!

Certain peculiarities, such as length, weight, or age, make them record breakers, but other aspects can also be noted.

A huge SUNFLOWER

SUNFLOWERS ARE VERY TALL FLOWERS, BUT IN GERMANY A TRULY GIANT ONE WAS HARVESTED: IT MEASURED 27 FT (8.23 M), ALMOST AS TALL AS A THREE-STORY BUILDING.

The BIGGEST fruit

THE FRUIT OF THE ENTADA GIGAS IS A HUGE POD EXCEEDING 6.5 FT (2 M) IN LENGTH AND CONTAINS 10 TO 15 LARGE HEART-SHAPED SEEDS.

The FASTEST

BAMBOO IS THE FASTEST GROWING PLANT SPECIES ON THE PLANET. IT CAN GROW UP TO 35.4 IN (90 CM) IN JUST 24 HOURS!

The SMALLEST fruit

IT IS PRODUCED BY A TINY AQUATIC PLANT *WOLFFIA ANGUSTA*. WITH A LENGTH OF .01 IN (.3 MM), THIS FRUIT IS SO SMALL THAT IT IS DIFFICULT TO DISTINGUISH IT FROM THE PLANT.

The SLOWEST

AMONG THE SLOWEST GROWING TREE SPECIES IS THE WESTERN THUIA. ONE SPECIMEN IN CANADA REALLY OVERDID IT: AFTER 155 YEARS, IT HAD GROWN JUST OVER 3.94 IN (10 CM)!

The THIRSTIEST

SOME PLANTS HAVE DROUGHT RESISTANCE THAT IS ALMOST MIRACULOUS: AN EXAMPLE IS *TILLANDSIA LANDBECKII*, A RELATIVE OF THE PINEAPPLE, WHICH GROWS ON SAND IN THE ATACAMA DESERT, WHERE IT MAY NOT RAIN FOR MORE THAN 100 YEARS.

The most DANGEROUS

THE TITLE OF THE WORLD'S MOST DANGEROUS TREE IS AWARDED TO THE SOUTHPAW, A PLANT WIDESPREAD IN THE CARIBBEAN. THE SAP CAUSES BLISTERS, AND THE INGESTED FRUIT CAN BE DEADLY. EVEN THE SMOKE FROM ITS BURNED WOOD CAN CAUSE SERIOUS EYE DAMAGE.

RAFFLESIA

SPEAKING OF FLOWERS, THE RECORD FOR SIZE BELONGS TO THE INDONESIAN *RAFFLESIA ARNOLDII*, A RARE LEAFLESS PLANT THAT ATTACHES ITSELF TO OTHER PLANTS TO SUCK OUT NOURISHMENT. ONE OF ITS STINKY FLOWERS CAN REACH UP TO 3.2 FT (1 M) IN DIAMETER.

HABITATS

-Chapter 3-

THE OCEAN DEPTHS

The abyss is the deepest part of the ocean, between 9,842 and 21,325 ft (3,000–6,500 m).

Below 656 ft (200 m), sunlight does not penetrate the water, so the world at these depths is completely dark.

The deepest POINT

THE CANYON KNOWN AS THE MARIANA TRENCH IS A CHASM OF MORE THAN 36,089 FT (11,000 M).

Underwater VOLCANOES

NUMEROUS VOLCANIC CHIMNEYS OPEN UP ON ABYSSAL SEABEDS, RELEASING ACIDIC FLUIDS AND GASES, OFTEN TOXIC, FROM THE EARTH'S INTERIOR INTO THE SURROUNDING WATER.

Hunting IN THE DARK

THE SPERM WHALE DIVES TO DEPTHS OF 9,842 FT (3,000 M) TO HUNT FOR GIANT SQUID. IN THE DARKNESS IT LOCATES THEM BY EMITTING CLICKS THAT TRAVEL LIKE SONAR WAVES AND THEN USING THE RETURNING ECHOES TO FIND THEIR LOCATION.

Special TASTES

DEEP IN THE OCEAN, THE AMOUNT OF FOOD DECREASES. IT IS NOT EASY TO CATCH PREY, SO SOME CREATURES MAKE DO WITH THE CORPSES THAT COME DOWN FROM ABOVE. MANY ABYSSAL FISH ARE SCAVENGERS, WITH MOUTHS THAT OPEN UPWARD, READY TO SCOOP UP FALLING FOOD SCRAPS.

What a SIGHT!

AMONG THE ABYSSAL "MONSTERS" ARE THE SEA SPIDERS, IMPRESSIVE FOR THE LENGTH OF THEIR LONG LIMBS, WHICH ARE DISPROPORTIONATE TO THEIR FAIRLY SMALL BODIES.

Tough CONDITIONS!

WITH NO LIGHT, VERY LITTLE FOOD, COLD TEMPERATURES, AND WATER PRESSURE THAT IS OVERWHELMING, ADAPTATION IS ESSENTIAL TO SURVIVE IN THE DEEP.

A world to EXPLORE

TODAY ONLY 5 PERCENT OF THE DEEPEST SEABED HAS BEEN CAREFULLY EXPLORED.

BLACK DEVIL OF THE DEEP

ANIMALS OF THE ABYSSAL DEPTHS, SUCH AS THIS ANGLERFISH, CAN BE TRULY FRIGHTENING WITH THEIR BULGING EYES, HUGE JAWS ARMED WITH LONG, SHARP TEETH, AND APPENDAGES WITH GLOWING ELEMENTS.

THE MOUNTAINS

A mountain is an elevation that rises above 1,968 ft (600 m).

All mountains are constantly changing environments. As you go up in elevation, trees are gradually replaced by smaller and smaller species until they disappear altogether. The animals that live at various heights are also different.

Record-breaking CHAINS!

WHEN CONNECTED TOGETHER, MOUNTAINS FORM "CHAINS." THE LONGEST MOUNTAIN RANGE IS THE MID-ATLANTIC RIDGE; 90 PERCENT OF IT LIES UNDER THE OCEAN! IN CONTRAST, THE ANDES ARE THE LONGEST CHAIN ON LAND: THEY RUN ALONG THE ENTIRE WESTERN COAST OF SOUTH AMERICA.

Experienced CLIMBERS

STEEP ROCK WALLS DO NOT PREVENT ANIMALS LIKE IBEXES FROM CLIMBING WITH AGILITY. THEIR SECRET IS IN THEIR HOOVES, WHICH PROVIDE A SECURE GRIP BECAUSE THEY HAVE A VERY HARD EDGE BUT ARE SOFT ON THE INSIDE.

The highest OF ALL

MOUNT EVEREST IS THE WORLD'S HIGHEST MOUNTAIN ABOVE SEA LEVEL. IT REACHES 29,032 FT (8,849 M), A HEIGHT EQUIVALENT TO A BUILDING THAT IS 3,000 STORIES TALL!

K2

THE SUMMIT OF THE SECOND HIGHEST MOUNTAIN ON EARTH, AFTER EVEREST, WAS FIRST REACHED ON JULY 31, 1954, AFTER MANY EXPEDITIONS HAD FAILED.

From forests to GLACIERS

AT MID-LATITUDES, MOUNTAINS HAVE VEGETATION DIVIDED INTO FIVE BELTS THAT FROM THE BOTTOM TO THE TOP ARE: DECIDUOUS FORESTS, CONIFEROUS FORESTS, SHRUBS AND BUSHES, EXPANSES OF GRASS, AND FINALLY MOSSES AND LICHENS. ON THE HIGH PEAKS, HOWEVER, THERE ARE ONLY GLACIERS AND ROCK.

A perfect ADAPTATION

THE SNOW LEOPARD'S BODY IS PERFECTLY ADAPTED TO LIFE AT HIGH ALTITUDES: ITS WIDE PAWS PREVENT IT FROM SINKING INTO THE SNOWPACK, ITS SMALL EARS PREVENT EXCESSIVE HEAT LOSS, AND ITS LARGE NOSE WARMS THE AIR BEFORE IT REACHES THE LUNGS.

A slow CREATION

MOUNTAIN RANGES CAN BE THOUGHT OF AS WRINKLES IN EARTH'S CRUST THAT, UNDER CERTAIN CONDITIONS, HAVE CRUMPLED UP AND RISEN. THEIR FORMATION TAKES SEVERAL MILLION YEARS.

Winter IS COMING!

SOME MOUNTAIN ANIMALS SURVIVE THE WINTER BY HIDING IN GROUPS IN UNDERGROUND BURROWS AND HIBERNATING ALL TOGETHER. OTHERS CHANGE THEIR APPEARANCE WITH THE SEASONS. FOR EXAMPLE, IN SUMMER STOATS HAVE BROWN FUR, WHICH TURNS SNOW WHITE IN WINTER TO BETTER BLEND IN WITH THE ENVIRONMENT.

DESERTS

When thinking of deserts, it is easy to imagine terribly hot and inhospitable places where life is almost absent.

This, however, is only part of the truth. Deserts can be environments of great beauty, made up of amazing landscapes and colors, with incredible creatures that have made their home here by struggling against adversity.

Is it a MIRAGE?

THE SCORCHING GROUND SOMETIMES HEATS THE AIR SO MUCH THAT IT RISES IN SHIMMERING WAVES, CAUSING US TO SEE DISTORTED IMAGES IN THE DISTANCE. IT IS THE PHENOMENON WE CALL A MIRAGE.

Dunes in MOTION

SAND DUNES ARE CREATED BY THE WIND, WHICH ALSO CAUSES THEIR MOVEMENT. IN FACT, THANKS TO WIND DUNES CAN CHANGE SHAPE AND EVEN MOVE DOZENS OF FEET A YEAR.

BRILLIANT Plants and...

DESERT PLANTS HAVE LEAVES THAT SPECIALIZE IN NOT LOSING WATER AND SPONGY STEMS THAT CAN STORE IT.

...ingenious ANIMALS!

THE SPINY DEVIL, AN AUSTRALIAN DESERT LIZARD, HAS AN INGENIOUS SYSTEM FOR COLLECTING WHAT LITTLE WATER IS AVAILABLE: IT HAS TINY FURROWS ON ITS HEAD THAT CARRY RAINDROPS AND DEWDROPS DIRECTLY INTO ITS MOUTH.

Life-saving HUMPS

CAMELS AND DROMEDARIES STORE FAT IN THEIR HUMPS. IN THE ABSENCE OF FOOD OR WATER, THEY WILL USE IT TO FEED AND HYDRATE THEMSELVES, THUS MANAGING TO LIVE LONG LIVES EVEN IN THE DESERT.

Very hot and VERY COLD

IN A DESERT, THE DIFFERENCE IN TEMPERATURE BETWEEN DAY AND NIGHT CAN BE REALLY BIG. IN THE CHIHUAHUAN DESERT IN MEXICO, IT CAN REACH AROUND 100 DEGREES FAHRENHEIT (40 DEGREES CELSIUS) DURING DAYLIGHT HOURS, WHILE AT NIGHT THE TEMPERATURE CAN DROP BELOW FREEZING.

NAMIB DESERT

THE NAMIB DESERT IS LOCATED IN THE SOUTHERN PART OF AFRICA, CLOSE TO THE OCEAN. FOR THIS REASON, IT IS COVERED DAILY BY A THICK FOG FORMED BY THE MOIST SEA AIR THAT REACHES THE MAINLAND.

Unexpected DESERTS

THE POLAR ICE CAPS ARE ALSO CONSIDERED DESERTS. IN FACT, ALTHOUGH THEY CONTAIN LARGE AMOUNTS OF WATER, MOST OF IT IS IN THE FORM OF ICE AND IS UNAVAILABLE.

The LARGEST

THE LARGEST HOT DESERT IN THE WORLD IS THE SAHARA, BUT IT WAS NOT ALWAYS SO. MORE THAN 5,000 YEARS AGO, THE CLIMATE HERE WAS VERY HUMID AND THERE GREW FORESTS POPULATED BY NUMEROUS ANIMAL AND PLANT SPECIES.

RAINFORESTS

Rainforests are a valuable resource for Earth because they are home to a wide variety of plants and animals, more than any other ecosystem in the world.

Most of them are located along or near the equator, where it is very hot.

From top TO BOTTOM

THE RAINFOREST HAS FOUR LAYERS: THE EMERGENT LAYER FROM WHICH THE TALLEST TREES SPROUT; THE CANOPY, RICH IN BRANCHES AND LEAVES THAT FILTER SUNLIGHT; THE UNDERGROWTH, MADE UP OF SHADE-LIVING PLANTS; AND FINALLY THE GROUND, WHERE IT IS QUITE DARK.

It's RAINING again!

IN A RAINFOREST THERE IS ALWAYS A LOT OF MOISTURE. BECAUSE SHOWERS OCCUR ABOUT 200 DAYS A YEAR!

A serious THREAT!

DEFORESTATION, OR THE FELLING OF PORTIONS OF THE FOREST, IS ENDANGERING THE SURVIVAL OF MANY RARE SPECIES. ON AVERAGE, 60 SPECIES OF PLANTS AND ANIMALS ARE DRIVEN TO EXTINCTION EVERY DAY IN RAINFORESTS AROUND THE WORLD.

A great RESOURCE

MANY PRODUCTS WE USE EVERY DAY COME FROM PLANTS THAT GROW IN THE RAINFOREST: NOT ONLY COFFEE, COCOA, VANILLA, RUBBER, AND FRUITS SUCH AS BANANAS AND AVOCADOS, BUT ALSO ANTIBIOTICS AND MEDICINAL SUBSTANCES EXTRACTED FROM SHRUBS, FLOWERS, SEEDS, ROOTS, AND MUSHROOMS.

VERY TALL TREES

RAINFOREST TREES BECOME VERY TALL BECAUSE THEY HAVE TO COMPETE WITH OTHER PLANTS FOR SUNLIGHT.

What DIVERSITY!

THE AMAZON RAINFOREST IS TRAVERSED BY THE WORLD'S LONGEST RIVER, THE AMAZON. ITS WATERS ARE HOME TO MORE THAN 3,000 DIFFERENT SPECIES OF FISH, WHILE THE FOREST IS HOME TO ABOUT 40,000 SPECIES OF PLANTS, NEARLY 1,300 SPECIES OF BIRDS, MORE THAN 400 SPECIES OF MAMMALS, AND MORE THAN 2 MILLION DIFFERENT SPECIES OF INSECTS!

The OLDEST

RAINFORESTS APPEARED ABOUT 300 MILLION YEARS AGO AND ARE THE OLDEST ECOSYSTEMS ON EARTH. AUSTRALIA'S DAINTREE RAINFOREST APPEARS TO BE 180 MILLION YEARS OLD AND IS CERTAINLY THE OLDEST OF THEM ALL.

SAVANNAS

The savanna is a flat grassland with scattered trees and shrubs.

We find it all over the world, but always near the equator. This habitat hosts a rich variety of both animal and plant life.

The GREATEST...

...AND ALSO THE MOST FAMOUS IS THE SERENGETI. THIS SAVANNA IS LOCATED IN AFRICA, IN TANZANIA, AND IS HOME TO MORE THAN 1.5 MILLION WILDEBEESTS AND HUNDREDS OF THOUSANDS OF ZEBRAS, AMONG OTHER ANIMALS.

Land PALACES

A CHARACTERISTIC FEATURE OF THE SAVANNA LANDSCAPE IS TERMITE MOUNDS. THESE LARGE TOWERS RISE FROM THE GROUND UP TO 23 FT (7 M) HIGH AND ARE VERY DURABLE. THEY ARE BUILT BY TERMITES TO REGULATE TEMPERATURE AND HUMIDITY INSIDE THEIR COLONY, BUILT UNDERGROUND.

Only two SEASONS

IN SAVANNAS THERE ARE ONLY TWO SEASONS THAT ARE DISTINGUISHED BY THE AMOUNT OF RAIN THAT FALLS. THE RAINY SEASON LASTS ABOUT SIX MONTHS, AND IN THIS PERIOD THE VEGETATION IS LUSH. WHILE IN THE DRY SEASON, BECAUSE IT RARELY RAINS, THE GRASS DRIES UP AND MANY ANIMALS ARE FORCED TO MIGRATE.

A big DECREASE!

THE LARGE ANIMALS OF THE AFRICAN SAVANNA ARE ENDANGERED. IN THE PAST 30 YEARS, NOT ONLY HAVE GIRAFFE NUMBERS BEEN NEARLY HALVED, BUT ELEPHANT NUMBERS HAVE ALSO DECLINED DRAMATICALLY DUE TO POACHING AND HABITAT LOSS.

Useful FIRES?

IN THE DRY SEASON, IT IS NOT UNCOMMON FOR FIRES TO BREAK OUT. AS STRANGE AS IT SOUNDS, FIRES ARE ESSENTIAL FOR ECOSYSTEM SURVIVAL BECAUSE THEY HELP LIMIT THE NUMBER OF INVASIVE PLANTS, REMOVE DEAD PLANTS, AND PROMOTE NEW GROWTH.

Leaves for ALL!

BY "DIVIDING UP" THE AVAILABLE PLANTS EATEN FOR FOOD, UP TO 16 DIFFERENT SPECIES OF HERBIVORES CAN SAFELY COEXIST IN THE SAME AREA OF SAVANNA. ALL IT TAKES IS FOR EACH TO EAT LEAVES GROWING AT DIFFERENT HEIGHTS OR TO FEED AT DIFFERENT TIMES OF THE DAY.

Not only HERBIVORES

THE LARGE AMOUNT OF GRASS PROVIDES SUFFICIENT FOOD FOR ALL THE NIUMEROUS HERBIVORES: BUFFALO, ELEPHANTS, ZEBRAS, RHINOS, AND GIRAFFES. AND WITH SUCH LARGE PREY, THERE CAN BE NO SHORTAGE OF BIG PREDATORS, SUCH AS LIONS, LEOPARDS, HYENAS, AND CHEETAHS.

ACACIA

THE MOST TYPICAL SAVANNA PLANT IS THE UNMISTAKABLE UMBRELLA-SHAPED ACACIA. ON THE BRANCHES ARE LONG THORNS THAT HARBOR TINY STINGING ANTS, ALWAYS READY TO DRIVE HERBIVOROUS ANIMALS AWAY FROM THE TREE.

THE STEPPES AND THE PRAIRIES

There are environments with only wide expanses of grass; these are the prairies and the steppes.

In both, rainfall is not so regular as to grow a forest, but neither is it so scarce as to give rise to a desert.

A nourishing SOIL

PRAIRIE SOIL IS VERY FERTILE BECAUSE IT IS RICH IN NUTRIENTS DERIVED FROM THE DECOMPOSITION OF THE VERY LONG AND BRANCHING ROOTS OF THE GRASSES IN THE DEEP SOIL.

A home FOR MANY

PRAIRIES CAN FEED A GREAT MANY ANIMALS. IT IS ESTIMATED THAT AS MANY AS 80 DIFFERENT SPECIES OF MAMMALS AND MORE THAN 300 SPECIES OF BIRDS LIVE IN SOME PLACES.

Steppe or PRAIRIE?

THE STEPPES RECEIVE ENOUGH PRECIPITATION EACH YEAR TO KEEP THE GRASSES ALIVE, BUT NOT ENOUGH TO MAKE THEM VERY TALL. IN FACT, STEPPE GRASSES NEVER EXCEED A FOOT AND A HALF (HALF A METER) IN HEIGHT. IN PRAIRIES ON THE OTHER HAND, MORE RAIN FALLS AND THERE IS GREATER PLANT DIVERSITY, WITH HUNDREDS OF SPECIES OF GRASSES, HERBS, MOSSES, AND OTHER PLANTS.

Running in the PAMPAS

THE EXTENSIVE GRASSLANDS OF SOUTH AMERICA ARE CALLED THE PAMPAS. HERE LIVES THE GUANACO, THE LARGEST WILD REPRESENTATIVE OF THE CAMELIDAE FAMILY, WHICH, LIKE ALL LARGE PRAIRIE HERBIVORES, IS A GOOD RUNNER.

A bizarre NEST

IN THE ABSENCE OF TREES ON WHICH TO NEST, THE LITTLE BURROWING OWL USES ABANDONED UNDERGROUND BURROWS DUG BY OTHER ANIMALS TO LAY EGGS.

A danger FOILED

THE VAST NORTH AMERICAN PRAIRIES ARE HOME TO THE BISON, A HUGE BOVINE THAT ONCE ROAMED IN VAST HERDS. AFTER FACING EXTINCTION IN THE LATE 1800S, TODAY BISON LIVE MAINLY IN PROTECTED AREAS.

Dogs... OR NOT?

THE PRAIRIE DOGS THAT INHABIT NORTH AMERICAN PRAIRIES ARE ACTUALLY RODENTS. HOWEVER, THE CRY THEY EMIT WHEN IN DANGER IS REMINISCENT OF A CANINE HOWL, WHICH EXPLAINS THEIR NAME.

MUSTANG

THE PRAIRIE IS THE REALM OF MUSTANGS. THEY ARE DESCENDED FROM DOMESTIC HORSES THAT ARRIVED IN AMERICA WITH THE SPANISH CONQUISTADORS. SOME OF THEM, ESCAPED OR FREED, ADAPTED VERY WELL TO THIS ENVIRONMENT.

THE DECIDUOUS FORESTS

These forests are formed by trees with leaves that fall in the early cold of autumn, leaving bare branches.

We also call these areas, simply, forests. The more specific term "deciduous" means "destined to fall," referencing the foliage of the trees.

Before the LEAVES

DURING SPRING, WHEN THE CANOPY OF THE TREES HAS NOT YET FULLY FORMED, THE SUN'S RAYS COME TO ILLUMINATE THE GROUND, AND THIS ALLOWS THE GROWTH OF MANY WILDFLOWERS THAT WILL BLOOM AS SOON AS LEAVES SPROUT ON THE BRANCHES.

Up or DOWN?

IN A FOREST, THERE ARE TWO LAYERS OF VEGETATION: THE CANOPY, FORMED BY THE FOLIAGE OF THE TALLEST TREES, AND THE UNDERGROWTH, WITH LOW SHRUBS AND A CARPET OF FERNS, MOSSES, AND LICHEN.

Farewell to the LEAVES!

LEAVES ARE TOO DELICATE TO WITHSTAND WINTER FROST, SO TREES DROP THEM BEFORE ENTERING A PERIOD OF "SLEEP." AS AN ADDED BENEFIT, THE FALLEN LEAVES DECOMPOSE AND ADD NUTRIENTS TO THE SOIL.

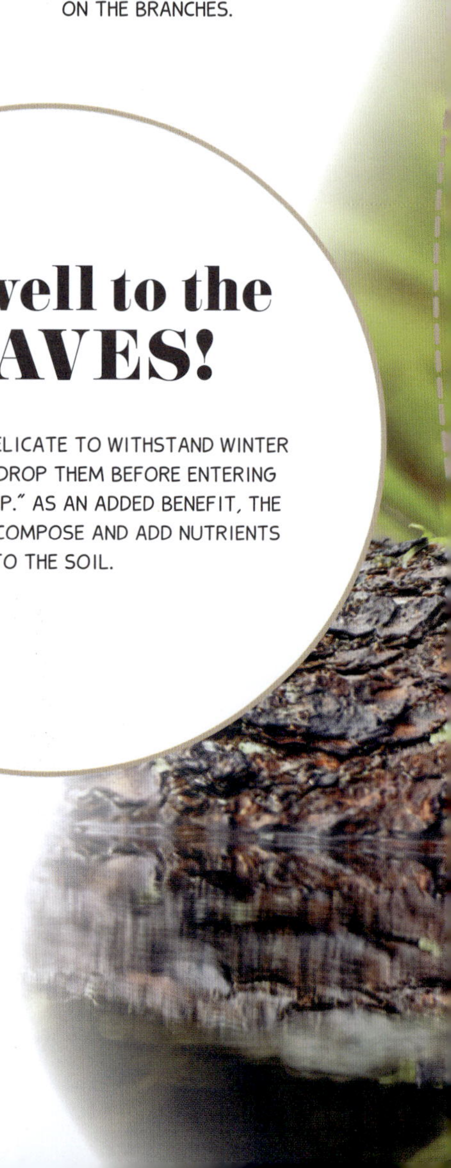

An intrusive INHABITANT

ONCE WIDESPREAD THROUGHOUT EARTH'S MID-LATITUDE AREAS, DECIDUOUS FORESTS HAVE OVER THE YEARS BEEN DESTROYED BY HUMANS WHO HAVE OCCUPIED THEM SINCE ANCIENT TIMES.

Some of them hate THE COLD...

MANY BIRDS AVOID THE COLD OF THE WINTER MONTHS BY HEADING SOUTH. WITH THE ARRIVAL OF SPRING AND THE FIRST WARM DAYS, THEY WILL RETURN TO FILL THE FOREST WITH THEIR SONGS.

...and some of them ADAPT!

SINCE THE ENVIRONMENT CHANGES WITH THE SEASONS, SOME ANIMALS HAVE DEVELOPED STRATEGIES TO COPE WITH WINTER, DURING WHICH FOOD IS SCARCE. SQUIRRELS, FOR EXAMPLE, COLLECT AND STORE ACORNS AND NUTS DURING FALL.

HEDGEHOG

THE HEDGEHOG SPENDS ITS SUMMER DAYS HIDING UNDER DRY LEAVES IN THE UNDERGROWTH AND BECOMES ACTIVE ONLY AT DUSK. FROM OCTOBER TO MARCH, HOWEVER, IT HIBERNATES.

With the cold weather, BETTER COVER UP!

FOR ANIMALS SUCH AS FOXES AND BOBCATS, THEIR WINTER FUR BECOMES VERY THICK TO KEEP THEM WARM.

CORAL REEFS

Coral reefs are underwater worlds full of vitality, built with architecture of delicate beauty.

They are so rich in animal and plant species that they are called the "tropical forests of the seas"! Here, creatures with some of nature's most bizarre shapes and colors dwell in delicate balance.

240 MILLION years ago

THIS IS THE VERY ANCIENT PERIOD WHEN CORAL REEFS BEGAN TO FORM. THOSE THAT EXIST TODAY ARE BETWEEN 5,000 AND 10,000 YEARS OLD.

WRECKER fish...

ALL THE FINE CORAL SAND IS MADE THANKS TO THE PARROTFISH. EACH FISH SCRAPES AND CRUSHES THE HARD CORAL WITH ITS TEETH TO FEED ON THE ALGAE; THE RESIDUE IS THEN EXCRETED THROUGH THE INTESTINES IN THE FORM OF GRAINS.

...and polyp BUILDERS

THE MAIN BUILDERS OF CORAL REEFS ARE TINY CORAL POLYPS. THEY PRODUCE CALCIUM CARBONATE STRUCTURES WITHIN WHICH THEY LIVE IN COLONIES. WITH EACH GENERATION OF POLYPS, THE STRUCTURE SLOWLY GROWS LARGER TO BECOME A REEF.

Cold BARRIERS

TO GROW, CORAL REEFS NEED LIGHT AND THE RIGHT TEMPERATURE. THAT'S WHY WE FIND THEM ONLY IN CLEAR, SHALLOW WATERS, AND ONLY IN THE GEOGRAPHIC RANGE AROUND THE EQUATOR, WHERE THE WATER TEMPERATURE NEVER FALLS BELOW 64.4°F (18°C).

Like a TWEEZER

THERE ARE 128 SPECIES OF BUTTERFLYFISH. THEIR SMALL, ELONGATED SNOUTS ARE VERY USEFUL FOR EXTRACTING CORAL POLYPS OR OTHER SMALL ANIMALS FROM THEIR HIDING PLACES.

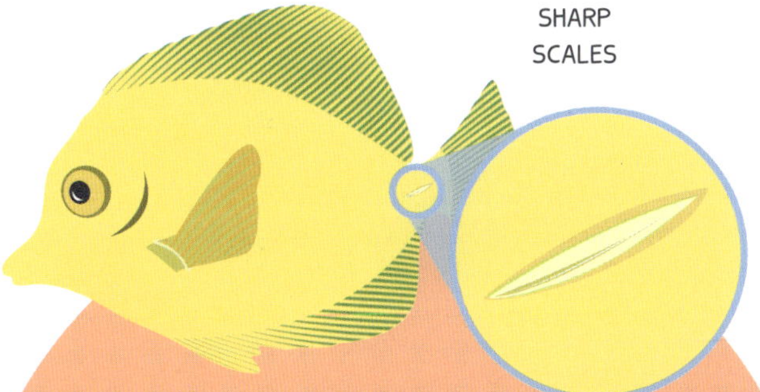

Don't make them ANGRY!

SURGEONFISH GET THEIR NAME FROM THE TWO SHARP HORIZONTAL SCALES ON THE SIDES OF THEIR TAIL. THE SCALES ARE LIKE SCALPELS AND ARE USED AS DEFENSIVE WEAPONS.

GREAT BARRIER REEF

THE GREAT BARRIER REEF STRETCHES 1,616 MILES (2,600 KM) ALONG AUSTRALIA'S EASTERN COASTLINE. AT 134 SQUARE MILES (348,000 SQ KM), IT IS THE LARGEST EXPANSE OF CORAL ON THE PLANET.

CAVES

A hole inside a rock large enough to fit a person is called a cave.

Caves can be natural or man-made, like mines. Some are found under Earth's surface or below sea level, others on mountain slopes or at the base of cliffs.

Cave SCIENTISTS...

...ARE CALLED SPELEOLOGISTS. THEY BELIEVE THAT THERE ARE STILL MILLIONS OF CAVES TO BE EXPLORED.

Work IN PROGRESS...

MOST CAVES ARE FORMED BY WATER PENETRATING EARTH THROUGH CRACKS AND FRACTURES AND DISSOLVING CERTAIN TYPES OF ROCK, SUCH AS LIMESTONE. THE WATER PASSAGES GRADUALLY BECOME LARGER OVER THOUSANDS OF YEARS UNTIL THEY BECOME CAVES.

What about in the sea INSTEAD?

SEA CAVES FORM WHEN THE CONTINUOUS MOVEMENT OF WAVES AND TIDES GRADUALLY WEAKENS THE REEF, ERODING THE ROCK INWARD.

Hidden in the DARKNESS

SOME ANIMALS SPEND THEIR ENTIRE LIVES IN THE DEPTHS OF CAVES. OVER TIME THEY HAVE LOST SKIN PIGMENTATION AND SIGHT, OR EVEN THEIR EYES SINCE THEY ARE USELESS IN THE DARKNESS. BLIND CAVE FISH, FOR EXAMPLE, HAVE NO COLOR, AND YOU CAN SEE THEIR MUSCLES AND INTERNAL ORGANS THROUGH THEIR TRANSPARENT SCALES.

Such SENSITIVE SKIN!

THE PROTEUS, OR OLM, IS A PINK-SKINNED AMPHIBIAN THAT DOES NOT METAMORPHOSE, LIVING WITH LARVAL PROPERTIES FOR ITS ENTIRE LIFE. IT HAS THE ABILITY TO PRODUCE PIGMENTS, AND IF IT IS EXPOSED TO LIGHT, THE BODY DARKENS.

Temporary TENANTS

SOME ANIMAL SPECIES, SUCH AS BEARS, OWLS, AND SWIFTS, TAKE TEMPORARY REFUGE IN CAVES BUT OCCUPY ONLY THE AREA NEAR THE ENTRANCE. BATS ALSO LOVE CAVES, WHICH CAN HOUSE UP TO 20 MILLION OF THESE SMALL MAMMALS.

STALACTITES AND STALAGMITES

INSIDE CAVES YOU CAN EASILY FIND ROCK FORMATIONS MADE FROM DRIPPING WATER. THOSE THAT HANG FROM THE CEILING ARE CALLED STALACTITES, WHILE THOSE THAT RISE FROM THE FLOOR LIKE MUSHROOMS ARE STALAGMITES. IF THEY COME TOGETHER, A COLUMN IS BORN.

FRESH WATERS

Freshwater environments include streams, rivers, lakes, and ponds, as well as swamps, marshes, and bogs, which are flooded or soggy most of the year.

These environments are absolutely essential for terrestrial life, as they are a storehouse of precious drinking water for all living things.

So FEW!

ALTHOUGH FOUND ON EVERY CONTINENT EXCEPT ANTARCTICA, FRESHWATER HABITATS MAKE UP LESS THAN 1 PERCENT OF THE PLANET'S TOTAL SURFACE AREA. THEY ARE CONTINUALLY REPLENISHED BY RAIN AND SNOW, OR BY THE MELTING OF HIGH MOUNTAIN GLACIERS AND SNOWFIELDS.

Continuous CYCLE

THE LIFE OF A RIVER BEGINS IN THE MOUNTAINS FROM A SPRING OR BY MELTING SNOW AND ICE. RIVERS OFTEN MERGE WITH OTHER RIVERS ALONG THE WAY OR FORM LAKES, BUT THEIR WATER ALWAYS ENDS UP IN A SEA OR OCEAN.

Lovers of CLEANLINESS

PLANTS SUCH AS ALGAE, WATER LILIES, QUAKING ASPENS, AND WILLOWS HELP KEEP WATER CLEAN BY USING THEIR ROOTS TO FILTER EXCESS POLLUTANTS AND NUTRIENTS FROM THE WATER.

Aquatic RECORDS

THE WORLD'S LONGEST RIVER IS THE AMAZON IN BRAZIL, WHILE THE LARGEST LAKE IS LAKE BAIKAL IN SIBERIA.

PANORAMIC homes

MANY BIRDS BUILD THEIR NESTS IN THE VEGETATION GROWING ALONGSIDE FRESHWATER EXPANSES.

What a CROWD!

FIFTY PERCENT OF KNOWN FISH SPECIES LIVE IN FRESHWATER ENVIRONMENTS. THEY LIVE AMONG SNAILS, WORMS, TURTLES, FROGS, MARSH BIRDS, MOLLUSKS, SHRIMP, ALLIGATORS, BEAVERS, OTTERS, SNAKES, AND MANY, MANY KINDS OF INSECTS.

NIAGARA FALLS

WHEN A RIVER TAKES A LEAP INTO THE VOID, A WATERFALL AND A NATURAL POOL BELOW ARE FORMED. LOCATED IN NORTHEASTERN NORTH AMERICA, BETWEEN THE UNITED STATES AND CANADA, NIAGARA FALLS IS AMONG THE MOST FAMOUS WATERFALLS IN THE WORLD BECAUSE OF ITS VASTNESS.

THE TUNDRA AND TAIGA

"Tundra" comes from a Finnish word that means "treeless plain," while "taiga" is a Russian word meaning "coniferous forest."

No tree species grow in the tundra, while conifers dominate in the taiga.

Welcome to THE TUNDRA

IT IS COLD IN THE TUNDRA: THE TEMPERATURE GOES FROM -40°F (-40°C) IN WINTER TO NO MORE THAN 59°F (15°C) IN SUMMER. THE GROUND IS COVERED WITH SNOW FOR MOST OF THE YEAR, BUT IN WARM WEATHER THERE IS AN INCREDIBLE EXPLOSION OF FLOWERS.

Long live THE SUMMER!

IN SUMMER, THE TUNDRA IS POPULATED BY VARIOUS ANIMALS SUCH AS REINDEER, CARIBOU, AND SMALL LEMMINGS, AMONG OTHERS. AT THE TOP OF THE FOOD CHAIN ARE CARNIVORES, LIKE THE ARCTIC WOLF, SNOWY OWL, AND POLAR BEAR.

Ponds GALORE!

DURING THE SHORT SUMMER THE SUN SHINES UP TO 24 HOURS A DAY, AND THE TOP LAYER OF PERMAFROST, THE UNDERLYING LAYER OF FROZEN GROUND THAT IS UP TO 3,280 FT (1,000 M) DEEP, MELTS SO THE GROUND BECOMES WATERLOGGED AND SWAMPS AND PONDS FORM.

White WINTER

WITH THE ARRIVAL OF WINTER, MANY ANIMALS MIGRATE SOUTH TO WARMER CLIMATES, WHILE OTHERS IMPLEMENT SURVIVAL STRATEGIES TO WITHSTAND THE LONG, FREEZING WINTER NIGHTS. THE FUR OF THE ARCTIC FOX CHANGES TO A SNOW WHITE COLOR, CAMOUFLAGING THE FOX WITHIN ITS ENVIRONMENT.

Welcome TO THE TAIGA

BETWEEN THE TUNDRA IN THE NORTH AND THE TEMPERATE FORESTS IN THE SOUTH IS THE TAIGA FOREST. CONIFERS DOMINATE HERE, SUCH AS PINES, SPRUCES, AND LARCHES, WHICH ARE EVERGREEN TREES ADAPTED TO WITHSTAND THE COLD.

The taiga CAT

THERE ARE NOT MANY LARGE CARNIVORES IN THE TAIGA BESIDES THE WORLD'S LARGEST FELINE, THE SIBERIAN TIGER. IT HAS THICK FUR AND A LAYER OF FAT THAT ALLOWS IT TO GET THROUGH THE WINTER WITHOUT ANY PROBLEMS.

REINDEER

THE ANTLERS OF THE REINDEER, ONE OF THE MOST COMMON DEER IN THE TUNDRA, FALL OFF EACH WINTER AND GROW BACK WITH THE ARRIVAL OF SPRING.

A strict DIET

WHILE MOST TAIGA BIRDS MIGRATE SOUTH WITH THE COMING OF WINTER, THE CROSSBILL ENDURES BY FEEDING ON PINE NUTS. ITS BEAK IS SO CROOKED AT THE TIP THAT IT LOOKS BROKEN. IN FACT, IT IS A VERY EFFECTIVE TOOL FOR EXTRACTING THESE SEEDS FROM PINE CONES.

THE ARCTIC

The Arctic occupies the northernmost region of our planet.

Unlike Antarctica, the Arctic is not a continent, but an ocean of ice.

From here on, IT'S ARCTIC!

SCIENTISTS CONSIDER ALL THE GEOGRAPHICAL AREAS ABOVE THE ARCTIC CIRCLE, AN IMAGINARY LINE SURROUNDING THE TOP OF EARTH, AS PART OF THE ARCTIC.

What clever FOXES!

ARCTIC FOXES HAVE FUR ON THEIR PAW PADS TO AVOID SLIPPING ON THE FROZEN GROUND. AT NIGHT, WHEN THEY SLEEP, THEY WRAP THEIR FLUFFY TAILS AROUND THEIR BODIES LIKE A BLANKET.

So many SEALS!

SEALS ARE VERY COMMON IN THE ARCTIC, AND THERE ARE SEVERAL SPECIES, SUCH AS THE BEARDED SEAL, RINGED SEAL, COMMON SEAL, AND GRAY SEAL. PROTECTED BY A LAYER OF BLUBBER, THEY SPEND A LOT OF TIME IN THE ICY WATER CATCHING FISH.

The singing CETACEAN

THE ICY WATERS ARE HOME TO MANY CETACEANS, SUCH AS THE BELUGA, WHICH IS CALLED THE SEA CANARY FOR ITS GIFTS IN "SINGING." BECAUSE IT LACKS A DORSAL FIN, THE BELUGA CAN CROSS NARROW CHANNELS AND CRACKS IN THE ICE WITH EASE.

SUN at midnight?

BECAUSE OF THE TILT OF EARTH'S AXIS, AT THE NORTH POLE IN WINTER THE SUN DISAPPEARS FOR SIX MONTHS. THIS IS THE LONG POLAR NIGHT. FROM MARCH UNTIL SEPTEMBER, HOWEVER, THE SUN DOES NOT SET AND CAN BE SEEN SHINING ABOVE THE HORIZON AT MIDNIGHT.

Penguins? NOPE!

THERE ARE MANY ANIMALS IN THE ARCTIC, SUCH AS FULMARS (A TYPE OF SEABIRD), MUSK OXEN, AND GROUND BEETLES, BUT CERTAINLY NOT PENGUINS, WHICH LIVE ONLY IN THE SOUTHERN HEMISPHERE.

The biggest PREDATOR

POLAR BEARS, THE LARGEST TERRESTRIAL PREDATORS ON EARTH, ARE CLASSIFIED AS HYPERCARNIVORES BECAUSE THEIR DIET CONSISTS MAINLY OF MEAT, OFTEN SEAL MEAT, WHICH THEY HUNT WITH CUNNING AND SKILL.

CLIMATE CHANGE

DUE TO CLIMATE CHANGE, THE ICE COVER IS SLOWLY RETREATING, AND IF ESTIMATES ARE CORRECT, TOTAL MELTING WILL CAUSE A 24 FT (7.3 M) RISE IN SEA LEVEL.

ANTARCTICA

Antarctica is one of the seven continents, and probably the most mysterious.

Far from inhabited lands and with a terribly cold climate, Antarctica has never been populated by people, and today only a few scientists live there permanently.

HUGE!

ANTARCTICA HAS AN AREA OF MORE THAN 5.4 MILLION SQUARE MILES (14 MILLION SQ KM) AND IS NEARLY TWICE THE SIZE OF AUSTRALIA.

How HOT!

OVER THE PAST 50 YEARS, AVERAGE TEMPERATURES ON THIS CONTINENT HAVE INCREASED FIVE TIMES MORE THAN THE PLANET'S AVERAGE.

LARGE and small

THE OCEAN SURROUNDING ANTARCTICA IS HOME TO PHYTOPLANKTON, WHICH ARE THE SMALLEST AND OLDEST LIVING THINGS ON THE PLANET AND RANGE IN SIZE FROM 2 TO 30 MICRONS. THIS OCEAN IS ALSO HOME TO THE BLUE WHALE, WHICH CAN REACH 100 FT (30 M) AND IS THE LARGEST ANIMAL ON EARTH.

ANTARCTIC BLUE WHALE

0.51 in

THE LARGEST FULLY TERRESTRIAL ANIMAL ON THE CONTINENT IS A WINGLESS MIDGE *(BELGICA ANTARCTICA)*, LESS THAN 0.51 IN (1.3 CM) LONG. THERE ARE NO FLYING INSECTS BECAUSE THEY WOULD BE EASILY SWEPT AWAY BY THE WIND.

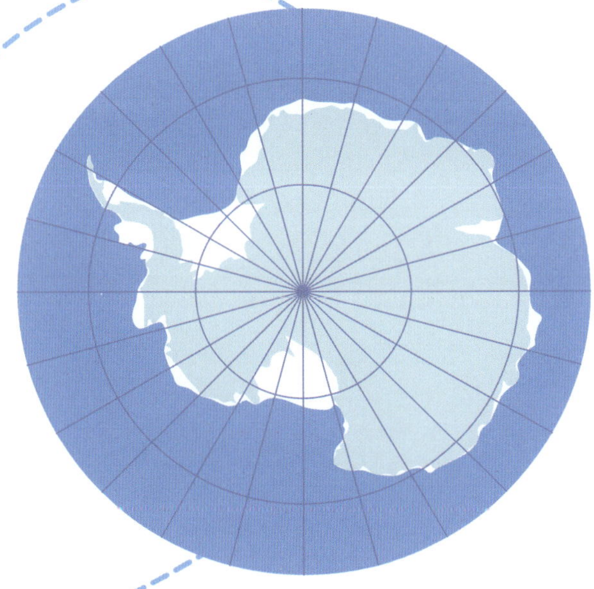

0.39 in

OVER THE PAST 30 YEARS, AN AVERAGE OF JUST 0.39 IN (10 MM) OF RAIN OR SNOW HAS FALLEN PER YEAR, A FIGURE SO LOW THAT ANTARCTICA IS CLASSIFIED AS A DESERT.

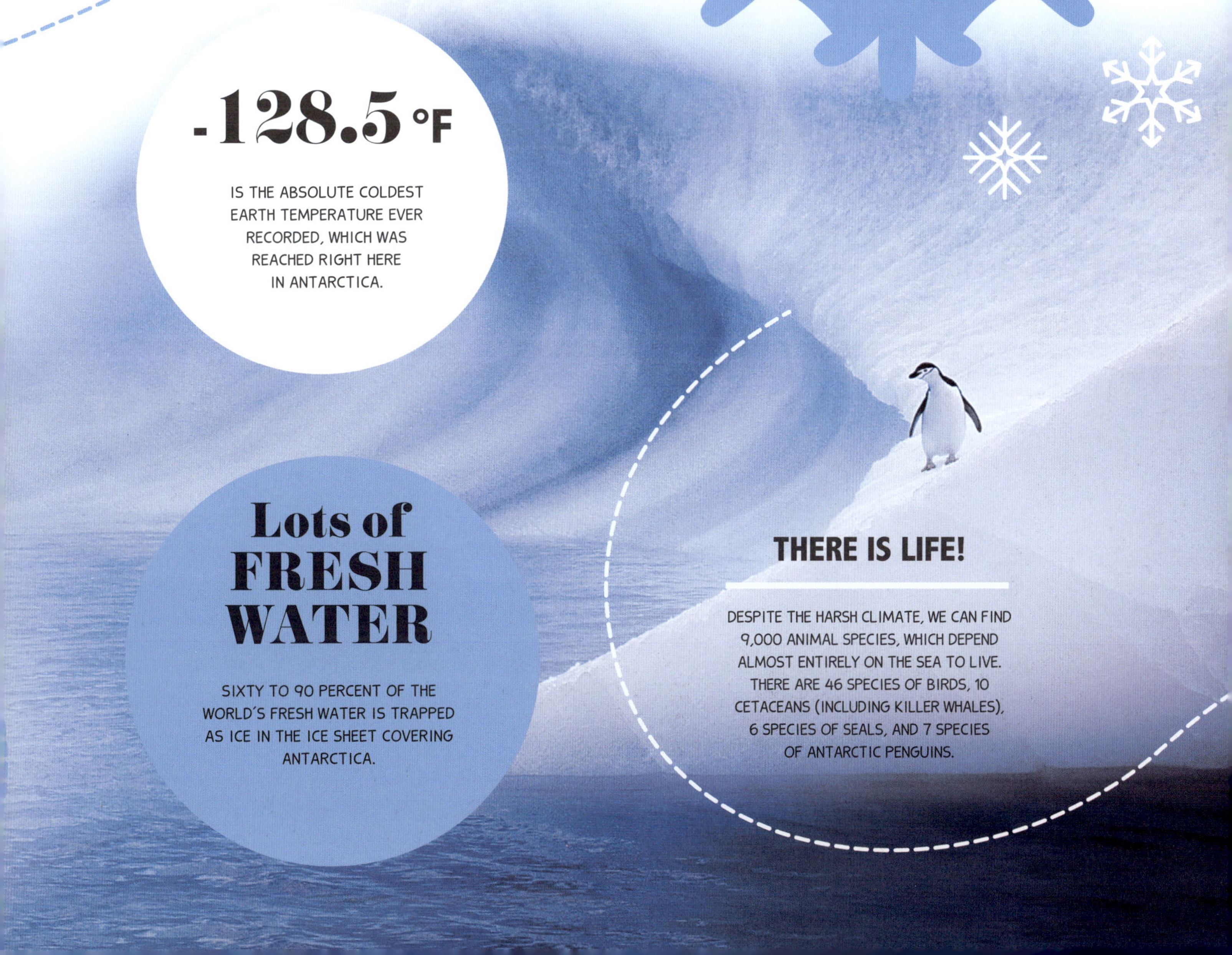

-128.5 °F

IS THE ABSOLUTE COLDEST EARTH TEMPERATURE EVER RECORDED, WHICH WAS REACHED RIGHT HERE IN ANTARCTICA.

Lots of FRESH WATER

SIXTY TO 90 PERCENT OF THE WORLD'S FRESH WATER IS TRAPPED AS ICE IN THE ICE SHEET COVERING ANTARCTICA.

THERE IS LIFE!

DESPITE THE HARSH CLIMATE, WE CAN FIND 9,000 ANIMAL SPECIES, WHICH DEPEND ALMOST ENTIRELY ON THE SEA TO LIVE. THERE ARE 46 SPECIES OF BIRDS, 10 CETACEANS (INCLUDING KILLER WHALES), 6 SPECIES OF SEALS, AND 7 SPECIES OF ANTARCTIC PENGUINS.

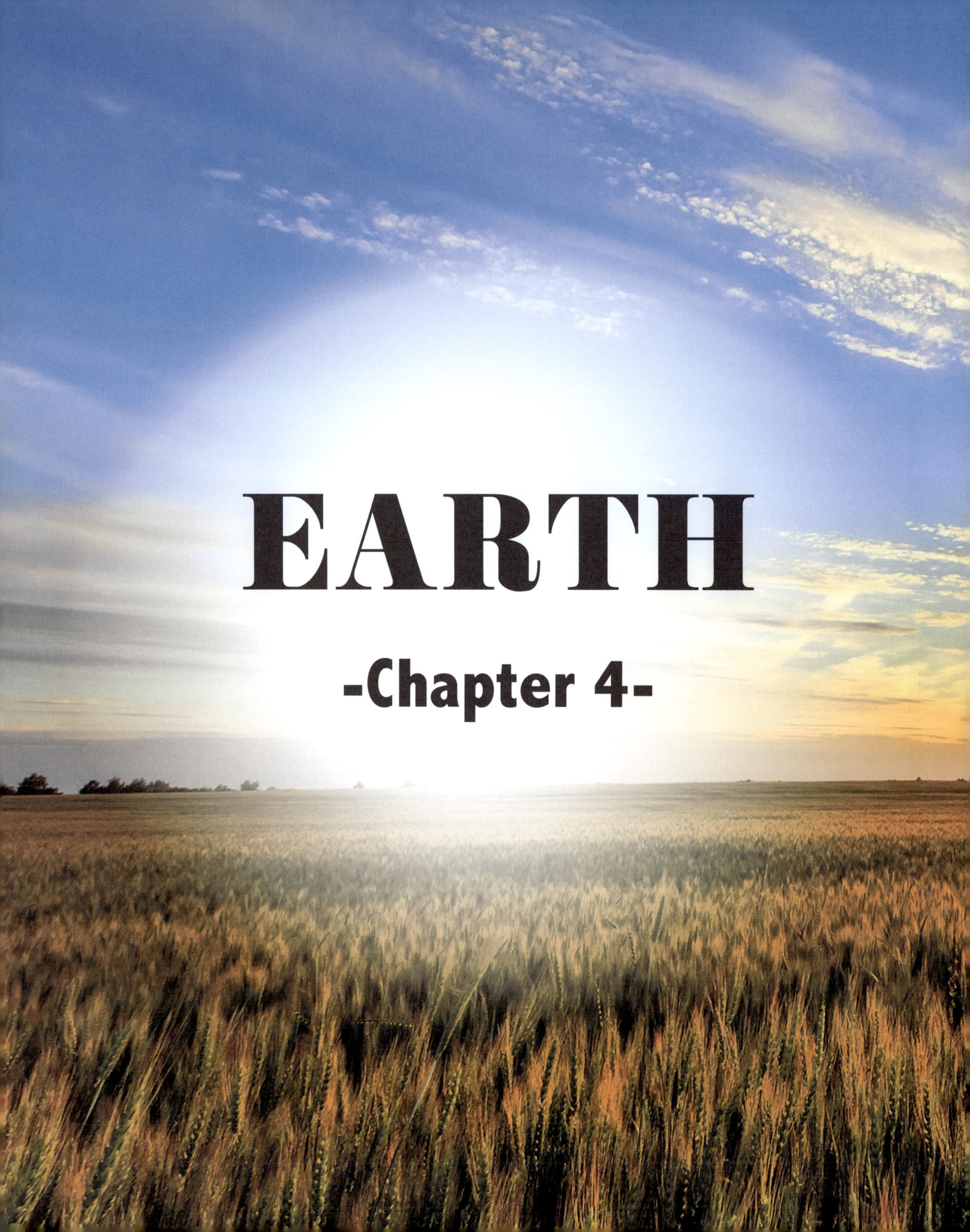

EARTH

-Chapter 4-

RAIN, SNOW, AND HAIL

Clouds are like reservoirs of water floating in the air.

Similar to sponges, clouds hold water droplets that they distribute in the form of rain, sleet, hail, and snow, which are all called precipitation. Through precipitation, water passes from the atmosphere to the ground.

The recipe for RAIN

WITHIN A CLOUD, WATER DROPLETS GATHER AROUND TINY DUST PARTICLES AND SLOWLY GROW LARGER. WHEN THEY BECOME TOO HEAVY TO REMAIN SUSPENDED IN THE AIR, THEY FALL TO THE GROUND.

Up and down inside a CLOUD!

WHEN CHUNKS OF ICE FALL FROM THE CLOUDS, IT IS CALLED HAIL. THE FORMATION OF A HAILSTONE OCCURS INSIDE A VERY HIGH CLOUD CALLED A CUMULONIMBUS. BECAUSE OF BOTH GRAVITY AND STRONG INTERNAL CURRENTS INSIDE THE CLOUD, ICE PARTICLES MOVE UP AND DOWN INSIDE THE CLOUD, ACCUMULATING A LAYER OF ICE WITH EACH PASSAGE. WHEN THEY BECOME TOO HEAVY, THEY FALL TO EARTH.

The true shape of RAIN

RAINDROPS DO NOT LOOK LIKE TEARS BUT LIKE SMALL SPHERES. THE LARGEST ONES, WHEN THEY FALL, LOOK LIKE A HAMBURGER BUN WITH THE FLAT SIDE FACING DOWN.

What BIG hail!

THE LARGEST KNOWN HAILSTONE FELL IN THE UNITED STATES AND WAS ABOUT THE SIZE OF A BASKETBALL.

LIGHTNING fast and hot

THUNDERSTORMS ARE OFTEN ACCOMPANIED BY LIGHTNING, WHICH ARE DISCHARGES OF ELECTRICITY INTO THE ATMOSPHERE THAT CAN REACH EXTREMELY HIGH TEMPERATURES AND INCREDIBLE SPEED!

No two flakes ARE ALIKE!

IF DROPLETS IN THE CLOUDS FREEZE, SNOWFLAKES FORM. AS THEY FALL FROM THE SKY TO THE GROUND, EACH SNOWFLAKE FOLLOWS A SLIGHTLY DIFFERENT PATH. THIS CAUSES THE ICE THEY ARE MADE OF TO BE ARRANGES IN VARIOUS WAYS, MAKING EACH FLAKE DIFFERENT.

Snow? NO! SLEET

SLEET IS SOMETHING DIFFERENT FROM SNOW. IT FORMS WHEN SNOWFLAKES PARTIALLY MELT AND REFREEZE INTO TINY ICE BALLS THAT FALL FASTER THAN SNOWFLAKES BEFORE THEY HIT THE GROUND.

SNOWMAN

THE HIISTORY OF MAKING SNOWMEN IN THE WINTER IS UNCLEAR, BUT IT HAS BEEN DOCUMENTED SINCE THE MIDDLE AGES.

WINDS AND CLOUDS

White, thick, and fluffy, or low, gray, and thin—clouds take many different shapes in the sky.

Clouds are moved by the wind, constantly changing shape. They can also form layers so vast that they cover the sky for days.

How is WIND created?

WINDS ARE THE MOVEMENT OF AIR FROM ONE PLACE TO ANOTHER. IN AREAS THAT ARE MORE DIRECTLY SUBJECTED TO SOLAR HEATING, THE AIR BECOMES WARMER AND RISES UPWARD, LEAVING A VOID THAT IS IMMEDIATELY FILLED. THE DISPLACEMENT OF THESE AIR MASSES IS THE WIND.

With the wind in THEIR SAILS!

WINDS DO NOT ALL HAVE THE SAME STRENGTH. IN ORDER TO CLASSIFY THEM, ENGLISH ADMIRAL SIR FRANCIS BEAUFORT INVENTED THE WIND SCALE IN 1806, IN WHICH HE ASSIGNED A VALUE FROM 0 TO 12, BASED ON THE EFFECT OF WIND ON SHIPS' SAILS.

CUMULUS CLOUDS

CUMULUS CLOUDS ARE THE MOST FASCINATING. THEY CAN BE SEEN ON WARM, SUNNY DAYS AND LOOK LIKE FLUFFY COTTON BALLS FLOATING IN THE SKY. THEY MAY TAKE THE SHAPE OF A CAT, A TURTLE, OR SOME OTHER CREATURE.

A PRICELESS resource

WIND POWER IS AN INCREDIBLE RESOURCE BECAUSE IT IS RENEWABLE AND CONSTANT. HUMANS HAVE HARNESSED IT FOR MILLENNIA TO CREATE ENERGY.

How a CLOUD is born

A CLOUD IS BORN WHEN MICROSCOPIC DROPLETS OF WATER VAPOR ARE CARRIED UPWARD BY WARM AIR. AS THEY RISE, THEY COOL TO BECOME WATER DROPLETS. NUMEROUS WATER DROPLETS SUSPENDED IN THE AIR MAKE UP THE "BODY" OF CLOUDS.

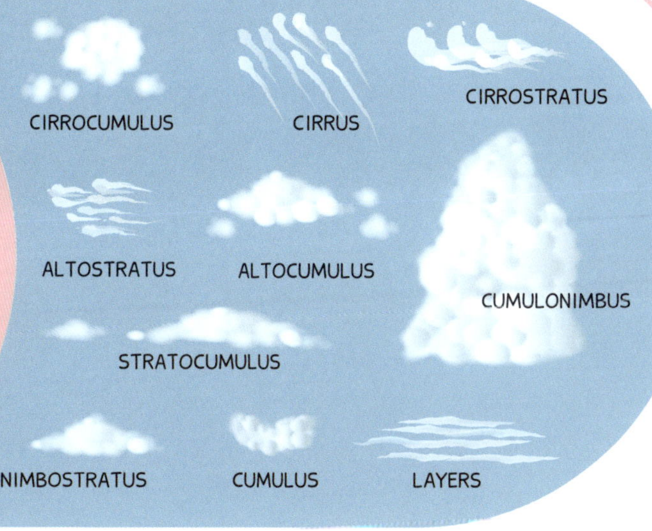

In COLOR or in BLACK AND WHITE

SOME CLOUDS ARE WHITE BECAUSE THEY REFLECT THE SUN'S RAYS. GRAY ONES, ON THE OTHER HAND, ARE SO FULL OF WATER THAT THEY NO LONGER REFLECT SUNLIGHT.

DROPS and droplets

WITHIN CLOUDS, WATER DROPLETS ARE MICROSCOPIC IN SIZE. SOME ARE SO SMALL THAT IT WOULD TAKE A MILLION OF THEM ALONE TO FORM A SINGLE RAINDROP.

THE COLORS OF THE SKY

Looking at the sky, we cannot help but marvel at the beauty of the colors that can be observed.

First and foremost is blue, with all its different shades, but there's also the red of sunsets and the somber hues of night. There are also many phenomena with such varied hues that they have always enchanted human beings.

The birth of COLORS

THE ORIGIN OF THE SKY'S COLORS IS SUNLIGHT, WHICH IS COMPOSED OF ALL THE COLORS OF THE RAINBOW. THE COLORS TRAVEL IN WAVES OF VARYING LENGTHS, FROM THE SHORTER WAVES OF PURPLE AND BLUE TO THE LONGER WAVES OF ORANGE AND RED.

Shades of the SKY

THE SKY IS NOT THE SAME BLUE COLOR EVERY DAY, BUT VARIES ACCORDING TO THE AMOUNT OF DUST AND DROPLETS IN THE AIR. WHEN THERE ARE FEW, THE BLUE OF THE SKY IS MORE INTENSE; WHEN THERE ARE MANY, THE COLOR BECOMES LIGHTER AND FADED.

Sunrise and SUNSET

DURING SUNRISE AND SUNSET, THE SUN IS LOW ON THE HORIZON. ITS RAYS, THEREFORE, REACH US BY PASSING THROUGH A LARGER PORTION OF THE ATMOSPHERE THAN WHEN THE SUN IS HIGH IN THE SKY. BECAUSE OF THIS, THE LONGEST WAVES OF LIGHT, NAMELY THOSE OF RED AND ORANGE, ARE VISIBLE.

The artistic ATMOSPHERE

WHAT DETERMINES ALL THE COLORS IN THE SKY IS THE ATMOSPHERE. IF IT DIDN'T EXIST, THERE WOULD BE FEW COLORS TO SEE OTHER THAN THE WHITE OF THE SUN AND STARS, AND BLACK ALL AROUND BECAUSE THERE WOULD BE NOTHING FOR LIGHT TO INTERACT WITH.

Ancient SKY

UNTIL ABOUT 2.5 BILLION YEARS AGO, EARTH'S SKY WAS ORANGE IN COLOR BECAUSE THE ATMOSPHERE WAS COMPOSED OF TOXIC VAPORS, INCLUDING METHANE. THIS GAS WAS PRIMARILY RESPONSIBLE FOR THAT HUE.

All the colors of the RAINBOW

A RAINBOW IS A SPECTACLE OF COLOR THAT APPEARS IN THE SKY AT THE END OF A THUNDERSTORM, WHEN THE SUN'S RAYS STRIKE THE RAINDROPS STILL IN THE AIR. THE WHITE LIGHT IS SPLIT BY THE DROPS INTO ALL ITS COMPONENT COLORS: RED, ORANGE, YELLOW, GREEN, BLUE, INDIGO, AND VIOLET.

An impossible TREASURE!

IT'S IMPOSSIBLE TO REACH THE END OF A RAINBOW BECAUSE IN REALITY ALL RAINBOWS ARE CIRCULAR. LOOKING AT THEM FROM THE GROUND, WE CAN SEE ONLY HALF OF THEM, AS AN ARC. FROM AN AIRPLANE WINDOW, ON THE OTHER HAND, WE CAN SEE THE WHOLE CIRCLE.

AURORA BOREALIS

IN THE FAR NORTH IT IS POSSIBLE TO OBSERVE THE AURORA BOREALIS, WHICH ARE UNDULATING RIBBONS OF LIGHT THAT ILLUMINATE THE NIGHT SKY. THEY FORM WHEN ELECTRICALLY CHARGED PARTICLES FROM THE SUN ENTER EARTH'S ATMOSPHERE, "LIGHTING UP" ATOMS LIKE NEON LIGHTS. THE NAME WAS CHOSEN IN 1619 BY ITALIAN SCIENTIST GALILEO GALILEI, WHO COMBINED THE NAME OF A ROMAN GODDESS AND THE ADJECTIVE "BOREAL," MEANING "OF THE NORTH."

HURRICANES

In different regions of the world they have different names: They are called hurricanes in the Atlantic, typhoons in the Pacific, and cyclones in the South Pacific and Indian Oceans.

After forming over the warm waters of tropical oceans, they roam for days with destructive power derived from rainfall and strong winds that blow in a spiral.

WHAT is your name?

HURRICANES ARE GIVEN HUMAN NAMES. THE WORLD METEOROLOGICAL ORGANIZATION PREPARES AN ANNUAL LIST COVERING 21 LETTERS OF THE ALPHABET AND ALTERNATING BETWEEN MASCULINE AND FEMININE NAMES.

5 categories

HURRICANES ARE CLASSIFIED BY THE STRENGTH AND INTENSITY OF THE WINDS THAT ACCOMPANY THEM. A CATEGORY FIVE HURRICANE IS VERY DESTRUCTIVE, WITH WINDS THAT EXCEED 155 MILES PER HOUR (250 KM/H).

WHEN?

HURRICANES FORM AT THE TIME OF YEAR WHEN OCEAN WATERS ARE WARMEST BECAUSE IT IS THIS HEAT THAT CAUSES MOIST AIR TO SPIRAL UPWARD. NORTH OF THE EQUATOR THIS OCCURS BETWEEN MID-AUGUST AND LATE OCTOBER, WHILE IN THE SOUTHERN HEMISPHERE THE SEASON RUNS FROM APRIL TO DECEMBER.

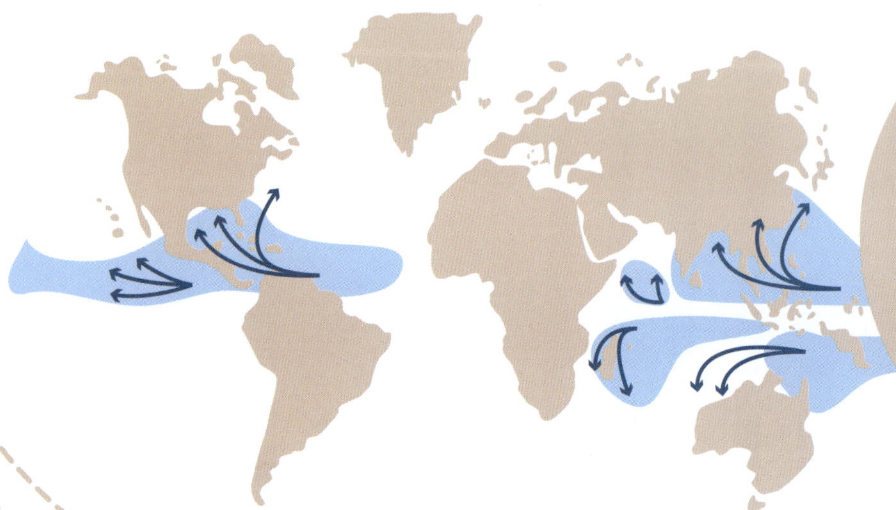

And WHERE?

HURRICANES MOVE AT A SPEED OF ABOUT 12.42 MILES PER HOUR (20 KM/H). KNOWING THIS VALUE ALLOWS SCIENTISTS TO CALCULATE THE TIME IT TAKES TO REACH LAND SO THAT PEOPLE CAN BE EVACUATED.

TWO WAY

DUE TO THE EARTH'S ROTATION, IN THE SOUTHERN HEMISPHERE HURRICANES ALWAYS ROTATE CLOCKWISE, WHILE IN THE NORTHERN HEMISPHERE THEY ROTATE COUNTERCLOCKWISE.

190 mile/h

THE LARGEST TROPICAL CYCLONE WAS TYPHOON TIP, IN 1979 IN THE PACIFIC OCEAN. IT REACHED A DIAMETER OF ABOUT 1,367 MILES (2,220 KM) WITH WINDS THAT BLEW AT 190 MILES PER HOUR (306 KM/H), FASTER THAN A SMALL AIRPLANE!

150

THE NUMBER OF HURRICANES THAT DEVELOP ON AVERAGE EACH YEAR. FORTUNATELY, MOST ARE OUT IN THE OPEN OCEAN AND DON'T CAUSE DAMAGE.

HURRICANE

AN IMPRESSIVE HURRICANE SEEN FROM SPACE.

TORNADOES

A tornado may be a small-scale weather phenomenon but it can be very destructive.

Tornadoes are funnel-shaped columns of air that rapidly spiral like spinning tops. Along the way they can uproot trees and lift all kinds of objects, even houses and cars.

The birth OF A TORNADO

A TORNADO ARISES WHEN COLD, DRY AIR COLLIDES WITH WARM AIR. THIS ENCOUNTER PUSHES THE WARM AIR UPWARD IN A ROTATING MOTION. A DARK FUNNEL-SHAPED CLOUD IS THEN FORMED THAT BECOMES LONGER AND LONGER UNTIL IT TOUCHES THE GROUND.

When they go to the SEA...

WHEN A TORNADO FORMS OVER THE OCEAN OR A LAKE, IT'S CALLED A WATERSPOUT. THE FUNNEL SUCKS UP THE WATER, REDUCING IT INTO DROPLETS, AND THIS USUALLY HELPS TO SLOW THE WIND SPEED.

...and when they PLAY with SAND

IN ARID AND DESERT AREAS AND IN THE PRESENCE OF A LOT OF DUST, A DUST DEVIL CAN ARISE. THIS IS A SMALL VORTEX WITH A MAXIMUM DIAMETER OF 33 FT (10 M) THAT FORMS DUE TO AIR TURBULENCE ON THE SUN-WARMED GROUND.

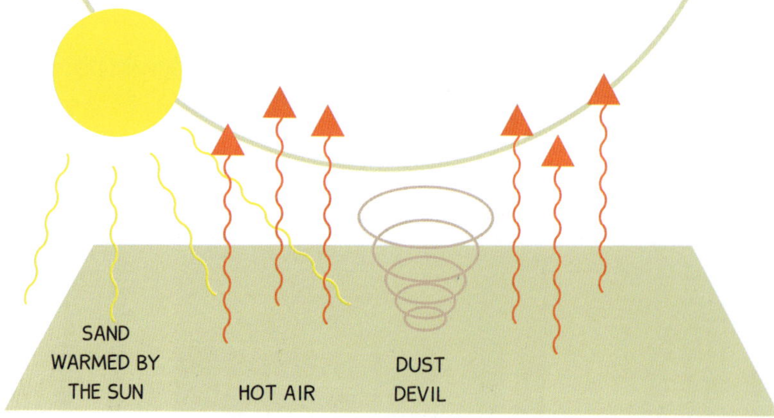

10 MINUTES or so

ALTHOUGH THEY UNLEASH ENORMOUS POWER, TORNADOES HAVE A FAIRLY SHORT LIFE SPAN, LASTING AN AVERAGE OF JUST 10 MINUTES, WITH A FEW RARE EXAMPLES EXCEEDING AN HOUR. USUALLY, THEIR END COMES WHEN THEY MOVE INTO COLDER AREAS OR WHEN THE CLOUDS BEGIN TO GET THINNER.

What STRENGTH!

INSIDE A TORNADO, THE SPEED OF THE SPINNING WIND CAN EXCEED THAT OF THE FASTEST RACE CAR. WITH ITS FORCE IT CAN OVERTURN TRAIN CARS AND SUCK UP ALL THE WATER IN A RIVER.

All of them in AMERICA?

TORNADOES CAN ARISE ALL OVER THE PLANET, BUT THEY ARE MOST FREQUENT IN THE UNITED STATES, WHERE ABOUT 1,000 FORM EACH YEAR.

TORNADO CHASERS

TORNADO HUNTERS ARE EXPERTS WHO TRAVEL TO AREAS WHERE TORNADOES FORM. WITH SPECIAL SCIENTIFIC EQUIPMENT THEY PHOTOGRAPH AND VIDEO TORNADOES AND COLLECT DATA FOR METEOROLOGISTS SO THEY CAN BETTER UNDERSTAND THIS PHENOMENON.

SEASONS

Seasons are a natural phenomenon that repeat every year and bring many changes.

In regions in the mid-latitudes-halfway between the equator and the poles-there are four seasons: spring, summer, fall, and winter, each lasting about three months.

What about at the POLES?

DURING ITS ANNUAL JOURNEY AROUND THE SUN, EARTH TURNS ONLY PART OF ITS SURFACE TOWARD OUR STAR, WHICH THEREFORE RECEIVES A DIFFERENT AMOUNT OF SUNLIGHT DEPENDING ON THE TIME OF YEAR.

In the SPRING

TEMPERATURES RISE, AND LIGHT RAINS FALL. PLANTS BLOOM, AND NEW LEAVES REPLACE THOSE THAT HAD FALLEN.

Wake up, lazy ones!

ANIMALS ARE ALSO AFFECTED BY SPRING. THOSE WHO HAD BEEN HIBERNATING COME OUT OF THEIR BURROWS; THOSE WHO MIGRATED NOW RETURN. FOR MANY IT IS THE TIME OF NEW BIRTHS. BIRDS PREPARE NESTS, AND THE EGGS OF MANY INSECTS BEGIN TO HATCH.

In WINTER

DAYS ARE COLD AND WINDY, WITH FEWER HOURS OF SUNLIGHT AND MORE HOURS OF DARKNESS. MANY TREES ARE BARE, AND VEGETATION IS AT REST.

So cold!

SOME ANIMALS COPE WITH THE COLD BY CHANGING THEIR FUR OR PLUMAGE, WHICH BECOMES THICKER AND WARMER. OTHERS SURVIVE THROUGH HIBERNATION.

REVERSED SEASONS

IN SUMMER, THE NORTHERN HEMISPHERE FACES THE SUN AND HAS MORE DAYLIGHT HOURS AND WARMER TEMPERATURES. CONVERSELY, IN WINTER, THE NORTHERN HEMISPHERE, TILTED TO THE OPPOSITE SIDE OF THE SUN, HAS FEWER HOURS OF DAYLIGHT AND LOWER TEMPERATURES. IN THE SOUTHERN HEMISPHERE, THE EXACT OPPOSITE OCCURS AND THE SEASONS ARE REVERSED.

In SUMMER

THE HEAT BECOMES MORE INTENSE, AND THERE IS GENERALLY LITTLE RAINFALL. TREES HAVE THICK CANOPIES AND BEGIN TO BEAR FRUIT.

What abundance!

ANIMALS EXPERIENCE THEIR BEST TIME OF YEAR. THEY HAVE PLENTY OF FOOD ON HAND, AND THE MORE PRESCIENT ONES STOCKPILE OR ACCUMULATE FAT IN ANTICIPATION OF WINTER.

In AUTUMN

THE HEAT IS GIVING WAY TO COOLER TEMPERATURES, AND THE DAYS ARE GETTING SHORTER. IN THE WOODS, THE LEAVES ARE TINGED WITH VARIOUS COLORS AND WILL SOON FALL FROM THE BRANCHES.

We must prepare!

MANY ANIMALS MIGRATE TO WARMER PLACES; OTHERS PREPARE A SHELTER WHERE THEY WILL SPEND THE WINTER.

EARTH'S CRUST

Earth is entirely covered by a very hard layer made of rocks and minerals that we call the crust.

The crust is quite thin compared to the size of Earth. You could look at it as the peel of an apple covering the fruit. It is crucial, however, because it provides an environment for all living things.

A broken CRUST!

LARGE FRACTURES DIVIDE EARTH'S CRUST INTO SEVERAL PIECES THAT FIT TOGETHER LIKE THE PIECES OF A PUZZLE. THEY ARE CALLED TECTONIC PLATES. THE PLATES MOVE ALL THE TIME, BUT AT A VERY SLOW PACE, COMPARABLE TO THE SPEED OF GROWTH OF OUR FINGERNAILS.

Powerful PLATES

TECTONIC PLATES ARE THE CAUSE OF IMPORTANT GEOLOGICAL PHENOMENA SUCH AS VOLCANOES AND EARTHQUAKES, BUT ALSO THE FORMATION OF MOUNTAINS, THE SHIFTING OF CONTINENTS, AND THE EMERGENCE OF NEW OCEANS.

A tense ENCOUNTER!

WHEN PLATES SLIDE OVER EACH OTHER OR COLLIDE, THEY CAN MAKE THE GROUND SHAKE, CAUSING EARTHQUAKES. THIS TENSION CAN BUILD UP FOR HUNDREDS OF YEARS AND THEN RELEASE ALL THE ENERGY IN AN INSTANT. IT'S KIND OF LIKE WHEN YOU PULL ON A RUBBER BAND AND THEN SUDDENLY LET IT GO.

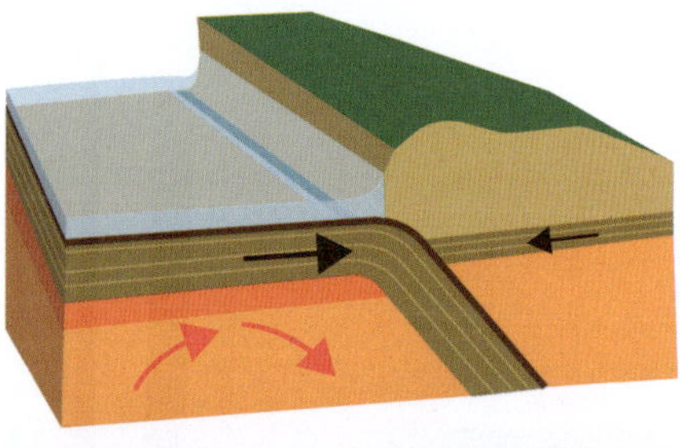

EARTHQUAKE vocabulary

THE POINT WHERE THE EARTHQUAKE BEGINS IS CALLED THE HYPOCENTER. IN CONTRAST, THE POINT ON EARTH'S SURFACE DIRECTLY ABOVE IT IS CALLED THE EPICENTER.

What level do they REACH?

TO CALCULATE THE POWER OF AN EARTHQUAKE, SCIENTISTS DEFINE ITS MAGNITUDE BY ASSESSING THE STRENGTH AND DURATION OF THE SEISMIC WAVES IT PRODUCED. EARTHQUAKES WITH A MAGNITUDE OF 5 ARE CONSIDERED MEDIUM STRENGTH, WHILE A MAGNITUDE OF 7 IS A MAJOR EARTHQUAKE.

Watch out for THE WAVES!

WHEN AN UNDERSEA EARTHQUAKE OCCURS, THE DANGER TO PEOPLE IS FROM THE RESULTING TSUNAMIS: GIANT WAVES CAN HIT THE COASTS, DEVASTATING EVERYTHING AROUND.

THE MOVEMENTS OF THE CRUST

NEW CRUST IS CONTINUOUSLY FORMED AROUND SOME PLATE EDGES, WHILE IN OTHERS, PORTIONS OF THE CRUST ARE DESTROYED BY ENTERING DEEP INTO EARTH, WHERE THEY MELT DUE TO THE VERY HIGH TEMPERATURE.

VOLCANOES

A volcano is much more than a smoking mountain. It is pure energy coming out of the heart of Earth!

They arise, in fact, when magma—a small part of the molten rock stored in the bowels of our planet—escapes from a rift in Earth's crust.

The CRATER

IT IS MAGMA'S EXIT DOOR. THERE IS USUALLY A MAIN ONE NEAR THE SUMMIT, WITH SECONDARY EXITS ON THE SLOPES OF THE VOLCANO.

LAVA

ONCE IT REACHES THE SURFACE, MAGMA IS CALLED LAVA, AND IT STARTS FLOWING DOWN THE SIDE OF THE VOLCANO. THE LAVA REACHES A TEMPERATURE OF 2,282°F (1,250°C), BUT THEN SLOWLY COOLS AND HARDENS, BECOMING ROCK.

AWAKE or ASLEEP

VOLCANOES CAN BE ACTIVE, DORMANT, OR EXTINCT. ACTIVE ONES ERUPT AT INTERVALS; DORMANT ONES HAVE NOT BEEN ACTIVE FOR SOME TIME BUT COULD STILL ERUPT. EXTINCT ONES, ON THE OTHER HAND, ARE INACTIVE AND WILL PROBABLY NEVER ERUPT AGAIN.

Blue LAVA

INDONESIA'S KAWAH IJEN, COMPOSED OF SEVERAL STRATOVOLCANOES, HAS A UNIQUE AND FASCINATING FEATURE: IT ERUPTS BLUE LAVA DUE TO THE LARGE AMOUNT OF SULFUR CONTAINED WITHIN IT.

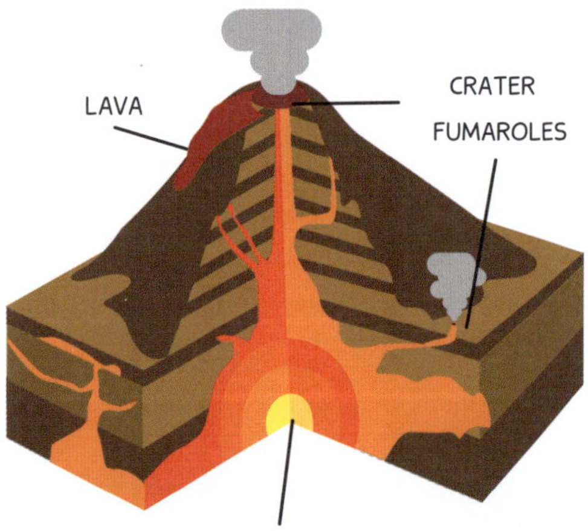

The MAGMA CHAMBER

IN MOST VOLCANOES, BEFORE RISING TO THE SURFACE, MAGMA IS STORED IN THE MAGMA CHAMBER.

STROMBOLI

STROMBOLIAN ERUPTIONS ARE MODERATELY EXPLOSIVE. INCANDESCENT LAVA IS INTERMITTENTLY EMITTED FROM A CRATER ON THE SUMMIT OF THE VOLCANO, GIVING RISE TO A LIGHT SHOW THAT IS VISIBLE ESPECIALLY AT NIGHT.

One year WITHOUT SUMMER!

IN 1815, THE ERUPTION OF TAMBORA IN INDONESIA LAUNCHED A COLUMN OF ASH AND HOT GASES INTO THE SKY THAT OBSCURED THE SUN. NO LONGER RECEIVING ENOUGH HEAT, EARTH FACED A YEAR WITHOUT A SUMMER.

1,500

THE NUMBER OF POTENTIALLY ACTIVE VOLCANOES IN THE WORLD. THE MAJORITY ARE CONCENTRATED IN AN AREA OF THE PACIFIC OCEAN IN THE SHAPE OF A HORSESHOE THAT IS CALLED THE RING OF FIRE.

ROCKS AND MINERALS

There are rocks and minerals everywhere around us because they are a fundamental part of Earth.

They make up Earth's crust, and since the planet began cooling billions of years ago, they continue to form. Generally, however, they break down over time due to erosion.

Classifying ROCKS

ROCKS HAVE DIFFERENT SIZES, SHAPES, COLORS, WEIGHTS, TEXTURES, AND STRENGTHS. THEY ARE CLASSIFIED ACCORDING TO HOW THEY WERE FORMED AND ARE DIVIDED INTO THREE MAIN TYPES: IGNEOUS ROCKS, SEDIMENTARY ROCKS, AND METAMORPHIC ROCKS.

Building MINERALS

MINERALS ARE THE BUILDING BLOCKS OF ROCKS. THERE ARE ABOUT 5,000 TYPES OF MINERALS, ALTHOUGH SOME ARE MUCH MORE COMMON THAN OTHERS. THEY OCCUR AS LARGE OR SMALL CRYSTALS WITH A CHARACTERISTIC SHAPE FOR EACH TYPE OF MINERAL.

Very slow ROCKS...

ROCK DEEP DOWN IN EARTH, LIKE GRANITE, FORMS VERY SLOWLY, AND THIS ALLOWS TIME FOR THE CRYSTALS TO GROW, WHICH ARE CLEARLY VISIBLE.

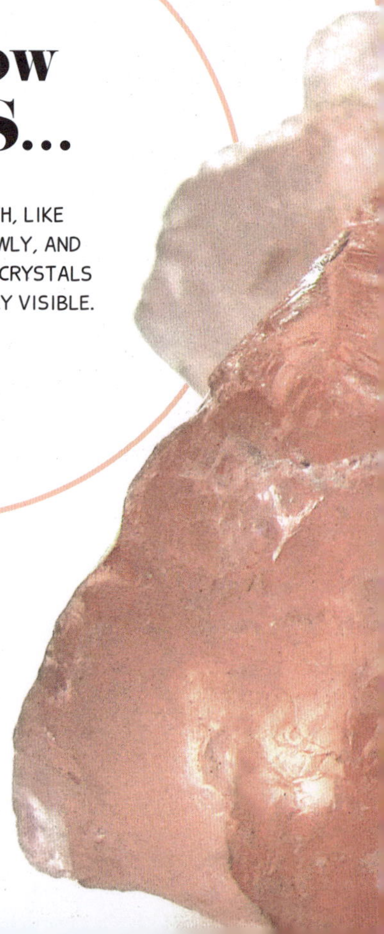

...and very fast ROCKS

FOR VOLCANIC ROCKS SUCH AS BASALT, FORMATION IS RATHER RAPID. BECAUSE OF THIS, THE CRYSTALS IN THE ROCK ARE VERY SMALL AND IN SOME CASES, AS WITH OBSIDIAN, COOLING OCCURS SO RAPIDLY THAT CRYSTALS DO NOT FORM AT ALL.

FLUORESCENT minerals

SOME MINERALS HAVE VERY CURIOUS QUALITIES. FLUORITE, FOR EXAMPLE, GLOWS UNDER ULTRAVIOLET LIGHT DUE TO A PHENOMENON CALLED FLUORESCENCE.

A most FRAGILE mineral

MICA IS A MINERAL THAT CAN BE BROKEN INTO SHEETS. ITS SURFACE IS SO SOFT THAT IT CAN BE EASILY SCRATCHED WITH A FINGERNAIL.

Fool's GOLD

THIS IS THE NAME BY WHICH PYRITE IS KNOWN, BECAUSE OF ITS DECEPTIVE GOLDEN APPEARANCE. IT WAS ONCE USED TO LIGHT FIRES BECAUSE WHEN YOU STRUCK IT WITH IRON, THE TWO MADE SPARKS!

The BUBBLE TEST

CALCITE IS A VERY COMMON MINERAL FOUND JUST ABOUT EVERYWHERE. IT CAN HAVE MORE THAN 300 DIFFERENT ASPECTS, BUT TO SPOT IT, YOU CAN DO THE VINEGAR TEST: POUR A FEW DROPS ON IT, AND IF IT IS CALCITE, BUBBLES WILL FORM.

QUARTZ

QUARTZ COMES IN DIFFERENT COLORS, FROM PINK TO YELLOW TO WHITE, AND IT CAN ALSO BE TRANSPARENT.

GEMS AND PRECIOUS METALS

All rocks are made of crystals, but not all crystals are precious stones.

Indeed, there are certain minerals and rocks that because of their rarity, durability, luster, and beauty are processed and turned into gems. Being highly sought after, they have a high value. Crowns of monarchs, pricey rings, and all kinds of objects have been adorned with them.

Rare, therefore VALUABLE!

THERE ARE METALS IN NATURE THAT ARE PRECIOUS BECAUSE OF THEIR RARITY, SUCH AS PLATINUM, SILVER, OR GOLD, THE LAST OF WHICH IS REGARDED WORLDWIDE AS A SYMBOL OF WEALTH.

A record-breaking NUGGET!

A PROSPECTOR TRIES TO MAKE A FORTUNE BY FINDING MINERAL DEPOSITS. THE LARGEST GOLD NUGGET FOUND TO DATE WEIGHED 72 KILOGRAMS (159 LBS). IT WAS DISCOVERED ALMOST BY ACCIDENT BY TWO MINERS IN FEBRUARY 1869 IN AUSTRALIA.

Similar, but DIFFERENT

ALTHOUGH IT IS MORE ABUNDANT THAN GOLD, PLATINUM IS MORE EXPENSIVE BECAUSE IT IS MORE DIFFICULT TO MINE AND PROCESS, AS IT MELTS ONLY AT VERY HIGH TEMPERATURES. SILVER, ON THE OTHER HAND, IS MORE MALLEABLE, WHICH IS WHY IT HAS BEEN WORKED FOR MORE THAN 4,000 YEARS.

Gifts from PREHISTORY

AMBER IS A PRECIOUS STONE THAT IS AT LEAST 30 MILLION YEARS OLD. IT IS DERIVED FROM THE RESIN OF PREHISTORIC TREES THAT FOSSILIZED, AND IT IS SO LIGHT THAT IT CAN FLOAT IN SALT WATER.

AMBER

What a RARITY!

ABOUT 200 GEMSTONES CAN BE FOUND IN NATURE, BUT THE RAREST IS MUSGRAVITE, DISCOVERED IN 1967 IN AUSTRALIA.

Animal "JEWELERS"

SOME GEMS ORIGINATE FROM AN ANIMAL OR PLANT. A PEARL, FOR EXAMPLE, FORMS INSIDE AN OYSTER, WHICH IS A MOLLUSK, WHILE RED, PINK, OR WHITE CORAL IS THE HARD PROTECTION OF SOME SPECIES OF POLYPS.

The TOUGHEST!

DIAMONDS

DIAMOND IS THE HARDEST MINERAL KNOWN AND CAN ONLY BE SCRATCHED BY ANOTHER DIAMOND. LIKE GRAPHITE IN PENCILS, IT IS MADE ENTIRELY OF PURE CARBON, BUT THE ATOMS ARE ARRANGED DIFFERENTLY.

The secret of the RUBY

WHEN CUT, A RUBY GIVES OFF A STRANGE OPTICAL PHENOMENON, MAKING A BRIGHT SIX-RAY STAR APPEAR WHEN THE STONE IS ILLUMINATED.

EMERALD

THE OLDEST DEPOSITS OF EMERALD, A BEAUTIFUL BRIGHT GREEN MINERAL, ARE FOUND IN SOUTH AFRICA AND DATE BACK NEARLY THREE BILLION YEARS.

THE MOVEMENTS OF THE OCEANS

The waters of the oceans are always in motion.

Ocean waters are pushed by currents, wash over the coasts as waves, and move up and down regularly, following the rhythm of the tides. Each movement is regulated by a change in temperature, salinity, wind, or the position of the moon in the sky.

Indispensable CURRENTS

CURRENTS ARE IMPORTANT BECAUSE IN ADDITION TO HEAT, THEY DISTRIBUTE NUTRIENTS IN MARINE WATERS, PROMOTING THE DEVELOPMENT OF PLANKTON, WHICH IS AN INDISPENSABLE LINK IN ALL FOOD CHAINS IN THE OCEANS.

Like rivers in the OCEAN

WHEN A CERTAIN AMOUNT OF WATER MOVES IN A SPECIFIC DIRECTION, A CURRENT OCCURS. THUS, CURRENTS ARE LIKE RIVERS AND CAN FLOW DEEP OR NEAR THE SURFACE, CAN BE WARM OR COLD, AND CAN ALSO BE OF SHORT OR LONG DURATION.

What an ATTRACTIVE moon

EVERY DAY THE SEA LEVEL RISES AND FALLS IN A PERPETUAL CYCLE DUE TO THE ATTRACTIVE FORCE OF THE MOON DRAWING SEA WATER TOWARD IT. LOW TIDE IS WHEN THE WATER RECEDES AND REACHES ITS MINIMUM LEVEL; WHEN THE WATER RISES TO ITS MAXIMUM HEIGHT, IT'S KNOWN AS HIGH TIDE.

The LARGEST and most FAMOUS

THE LARGEST CURRENT IN THE WORLD IS PROBABLY THE ANTARCTIC CIRCUMPOLAR CURRENT, THE ONLY ONE THAT GOES AROUND THE WORLD. THE MOST FAMOUS, ON THE OTHER HAND, IS THE GULF STREAM, WHICH FLOWS ACROSS THE ATLANTIC OCEAN, FROM THE GULF OF MEXICO IN CENTRAL AMERICA TO REGIONS OF NORTHERN EUROPE.

On the crest of the WAVE

WAVES ARE A FEATURE OF THE OCEAN. THEY ARE CREATED BY THE WIND PUSHING ON THE SURFACE OF THE WATER, CAUSING IT TO RISE. THE HIGHEST PART OF A WAVE IS CALLED THE CREST, WHILE THE LOWEST PART IS THE TROUGH. THE DISTANCE BETWEEN TWO CRESTS IS THE WAVELENGTH.

Cradled by WAVES

WAVES DO NOT MOVE WATER. IN FACT, AS A WAVE PASSES, A FLOATING OBJECT DOES NOT MOVE FORWARD, BUT RISES AND THEN RETURNS TO ITS ORIGINAL POSITION. ONLY NEAR THE SHORE IS THERE MOVEMENT OF WATER AS CRESTS FALL FORWARD, FORMING BREAKERS.

TIDAL WAVE

SOMETIMES ON THE HIGH SEAS, A ROGUE WAVE MAY SUDDENLY APPEAR OUT OF NOWHERE. IT CAN POSE A DANGER TO SHIPS NOT ONLY BECAUSE OF ITS UNPREDICTABILITY, BUT ALSO BECAUSE OF THE CONSIDERABLE HEIGHT IT CAN REACH.

FOSSILS

Sometimes traces of past life are found in the soil: a shell, a tooth, or a footprint—we call these fossil remains.

Fossils are important objects because studying them allows scientists to reconstruct what ancient living things looked like and how they lived. Thanks to fossils, we can learn more about Earth's long history.

How a FOSSILE is born

TO BECOME A FOSSIL, AN ORGANISM MUST BE BURIED BY SAND OR MUD, FOR EXAMPLE AT THE BOTTOM OF A SEA OR LAKE. IN A SHORT TIME, THE SOFT PARTS OF THE BODY DECOMPOSE, WHILE THE HARD PARTS BECOME STONE-LIKE IN NO LESS THAN 10,000 YEARS.

A SPECIAL ancestor

FOSSILS OF HUMANS' OLDEST ANCESTORS HAVE BEEN DISCOVERED. "LUCY," FOR EXAMPLE, FOUND IN 1973, WAS A FEMALE *AUSTRALOPITHECUS* WHO WALKED ON TWO LEGS IN THE AFRICAN SAVANNA MORE THAN 3.2 MILLION YEARS AGO.

The science of FOSSILS

THE SCIENCE THAT STUDIES FOSSILS IS CALLED PALEONTOLOGY. *PALEO* IS A WORD DERIVED FROM GREEK THAT MEANS "ANCIENT."

FOSSIL shells

THE QUEENS OF THE SEA IN THE MESOZOIC WERE THE AMMONITES. THESE MOLLUSKS WERE ABUNDANT, HAD SPIRAL-SHAPED SHELLS, AND SWAM BY JET PROPULSION.

One LAYER at a time

STRATIGRAPHY IS THE SCIENCE THAT ALLOWS US TO ANALYZE EARTH'S HISTORY THROUGH ROCK LAYERS. GENERALLY, THE LAYERS THAT ARE LOWER DOWN ARE OLDER THAN THOSE ABOVE THEM.

The language of FOOTPRINTS

FOSSIL DINOSAUR FOOTPRINTS CAN PROVIDE A LOT OF INFORMATION ABOUT THE ANIMAL THAT LEFT THEM, FOR EXAMPLE, IF IT WAS A PREDATOR, HOW FAST IT MOVED, AND WHETHER IT PREFERRED TO LIVE ALONE OR IN A GROUP.

T-REX POOP

EVEN POOP CAN BECOME A FOSSIL, IN WHICH CASE IT'S CALLED COPROLITE, WHICH MEANS "STONE DUNG." THE LARGEST COPROLITE KNOWN TO DATE IS SAID TO HAVE BEEN PRODUCED BY A *T-REX*.

Shells in the MOUNTAINS

FOSSILS ARE FOUND JUST ABOUT EVERYWHERE, EVEN ON MOUNT EVEREST, THE WORLD'S HIGHEST MOUNTAIN. FOSSILS FOUND THERE ARE THE REMAINS OF MARINE ANIMALS DATING BACK MORE THAN 450 MILLION YEARS. THEY ARE EVIDENCE THAT THE ROCK AT THAT TIME WAS AT THE BOTTOM OF THE SEA.

QUIZ IN 5 MINUTE

Test your knowledge and that of your friends by answering the following questions. Don't worry if you don't know the answers; you can find them in the book or in the solutions on page 175.

1

Do ocean fish drink? What about freshwater fish?

A YES
B NO
C YES AND NO

2

Which of these animals is poisonous?

A PLATYPUS
B GOOSE
C NEITHER

3

How long can kelp seaweed be?

A 328 FT (100 METERS)
B 164 FT (50 METERS)
C ONLY A FEW MILLIMETERS

4

Which ingredient is necessary for photosynthesis?

A WATER
B SALT
C CLAY

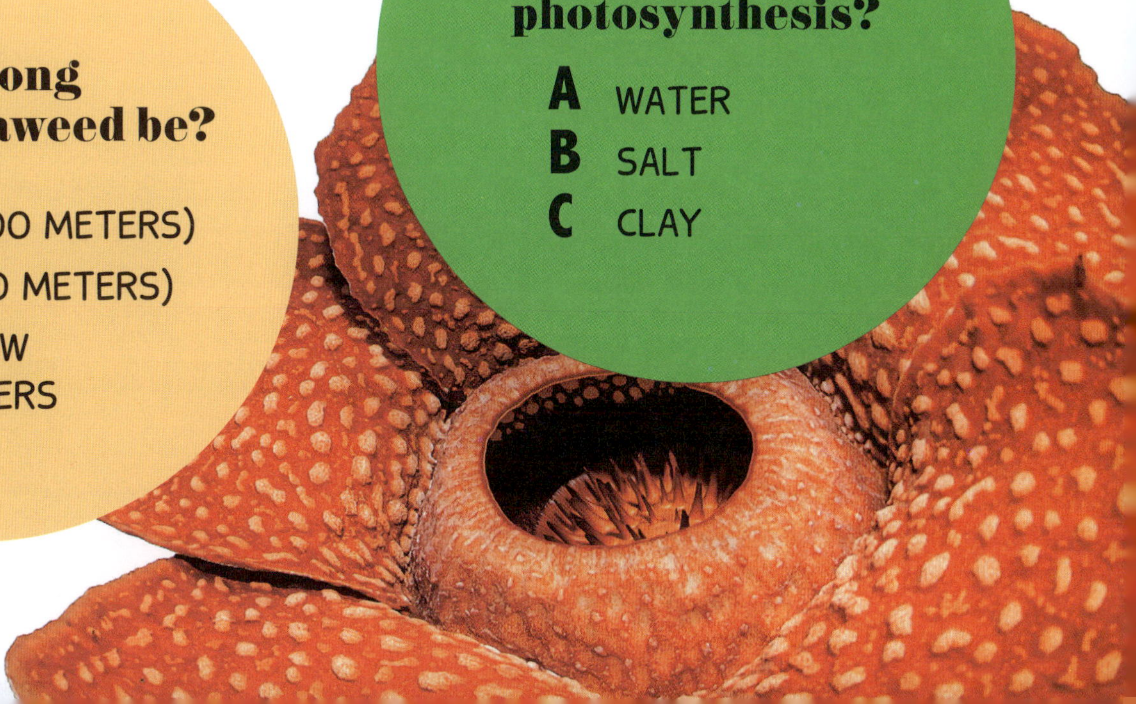

5

Is deforestation endangering the rainforests?

A YES
B NO
C IT WILL HUNDREDS OF YEARS FROM NOW

6

On average, how many hurricanes are there each year?

A 2,000
B 5
C 150

7

What birds live at the North Pole?

A FULMARS
B PENGUINS
C NEITHER

8

What was Lucy, whose fossils were found in 1973?

A *T-REX*
B *AUSTRALOPITHECUS*
C *BRONTOSAURUS*

SOLUTIONS

1-C **Yes and no**

SALTWATER FISH DRINK WATER TO COMPENSATE FOR THE WATER THAT IS EXPELLED FROM THEIR BODIES THROUGH THEIR GILLS AND SKIN DUE TO THE SALINITY OF THE OCEAN. FRESHWATER FISH ARE NEVER THIRSTY BECAUSE THE WATER NATURALLY PASSES THROUGH THEIR BODIES, THUS ELIMINATING THE NEED TO DRINK.

2-A **Platypus**

THE FRIENDLY PLATYPUS HIDES A SECRET IN ITS HIND LEG SPUR. IN MALE-TO-MALE FIGHTS, A PLATYPUS CAN WEAKEN ITS COMPETITOR BY INJECTING A POISON AND CAUSING IT SEVERE PAIN THAT LASTS FOR DAYS.

3-B **164 ft (50 meters)**

KELP IS A GIANT SEAWEED THAT FORMS UNDERWATER "FORESTS" AND PROVIDES FOOD AND HABITAT FOR VARIOUS OCEAN SPECIES, INCLUDING OTTERS AND SEA LIONS.

4-A **Water**

WATER NEEDED FOR PHOTOSYNTHESIS IS ABSORBED FROM THE SOIL THROUGH A PLANT'S ROOTS, WHILE CARBON DIOXIDE ENTERS THE LEAVES DIRECTLY FROM THE AIR. THE LAST, CRUCIAL INGREDIENT IS SUNLIGHT.

5-A **Yes**

DEFORESTATION, THAT IS, THE DESTRUCTION OF PORTIONS OF THE RAINFOREST, IS ENDANGERING THE SURVIVAL OF MANY RARE SPECIES. ON AVERAGE, 60 SPECIES OF PLANTS AND ANIMALS ARE DRIVEN TO EXTINCTION EVERY DAY IN RAINFORESTS AROUND THE WORLD.

6-C **150**

ON AVERGE, 150 HURRICANES DEVELOP EACH YEAR. FORTUNATELY, MOST HAPPEN IN THE OPEN OCEAN WITHOUT CAUSING DAMAGE.

7-B **Fulmars**

YOU CAN SEE MANY SEABIRDS AT THE NORTH POLE, SUCH AS FULMARS AND ARCTIC TERNS, BUT CERTAINLY NOT PENGUINS, WHICH LIVE IN THE SOUTHERN HEMISPHERE.

8-B ***Australopithecus***

LUCY IS A FOSSIL OF ONE OF OUR OLDEST ANCESTORS. FOUND IN 1973, SHE WAS A FEMALE *AUSTRALOPITHECUS* BARELY 3 FEET (1 M) TALL WHO WAS ALREADY WALKING ON TWO FEET IN THE AFRICAN SAVANNA MORE THAN 3.2 MILLION YEARS AGO.

Author

After graduating in natural sciences from the University of Milan, Cristina Banfi taught in various schools. For more than 20 years, she has worked in scientific communication and educational play and has enjoyed several editorial experiences in both scholastic and educational fields, particularly those dedicated to a young audience. In recent years, she has created several titles for White Star.

Photo credits

All photographs are by Shutterstock except the following:
Dreamstime: 2 top left and right, cover (bee); 2 center top left and center; 2 center bottom left; 2 center bottom; 2 bottom center.
Getty Images: 8-9, James Warwick; 19, Alberto Ghizzi Panizza/ Science Photo Library; 134-135, Georgette Douwma.

All illustrations by Valentina Figus.

Editorial Coordination
Giada Francia

Graphic design
Valentina Figus

Piazzale Luigi Cadorna, 6 - 20123 Milan, Italy
www.whitestar.it

Editing: Michele Suchomel-Casey

First printing, August 2025

ISBN 978-88-544-2163-9
1 2 3 4 5 6 29 28 27 26 25

Printed and manufactured in China
by Allied Fortune Times Limited (AF printing)
Dongguan City, Guangdong Province, P.R. China

FSC www.fsc.org MIX Paper | Supporting responsible forestry FSC® C178000